THE COINAGE OF
ROMAN BRITAIN

By

GILBERT ASKEW, F.S.A.

Second Edition

with an Introduction,
List of the Roman Governors of Britain,
and a Bibliography by

Peter A. Clayton,
F.L.A., F.S.A., F.R.N.S.

© 1951, 1980, Seaby Publications Ltd.

First published 1951   ISBN 0 900652 23 3

Second edition 1980   ISBN 0 900652 53 5

IVLIAE
CONIVGI CARISSIMAE
OB MEMORIAM IVVENTVTIS
QVAM LAETI SIMVL
PERIGIMVS.
G. A.

Distributed by B. A. Seaby Ltd,
11 Margaret Street, London W1N 8AT.

also

M. R. Roberts, Wynyard Coin Centre,
7, Hunter Arcade, Sydney, N.S.W., 2000
Australia.

Numismatic Fine Arts, P.O.B. 3788,
342 North Rodeo Drive, Beverly Hills,
California, 90212, U.S.A.

Whitman Publishing Co. Inc.,
1220 Mound Avenue, Racine, Wis., 53404,
U.S.A.

Printed in Great Britain by Pardy & Sons (Printers) Limited, Ringwood, Hampshire.

CONTENTS

INTRODUCTION TO THE SECOND EDITION

Nearly thirty years have passed since the first edition of Gilbert Askew's book, which sadly he did not live to see published. For almost two decades the book has been out of print but, nevertheless, always in use and of interest to the numismatist concerned with Romano-British numismatics. This continued interest in the book, reflected in the numerous enquiries for copies that the publisher continually receives, has prompted its re-issue as a second edition refurbished with a new Introduction, List of Governors of Roman Britain, and an up-to-date Bibliography. Gilbert Askew's text remains the same clear, concise guide with his characteristic scholarship and infectious enthusiasm for his subject. Had an endeavour been made to revise the text in its entirety this would have served only to delay the book's reappearance and to add considerably to its cost in an age when rising prices are a *sine qua non* for any book involving careful and complicated typesetting. Although new information has come to light in the intervening years concerning coin types that refer specifically to Britain, new coins of the 'British Empire' and, of course, the Carausius medallions, Askew's basic listing has stood the test of time and still provides the best easily available concise assessment of those coins of the Roman Empire relating to Britain and those struck by the usurper emperors in Britain at British or Continental mints.

In the last thirty years much has changed in Romano-British archaeology and numismatics. New sites have been found, notably the 'palace' at Fishbourne near Chichester which probably belonged to Cogidumnus, the Cogidubnus of the Chichester inscription who is hailed as king and imperial legate. Sites previously investigated have been subjected to fresh excavation and interpretation, notably Bath, Portchester Castle and Verulamium (St. Albans). 'Rescue archaeology', a phenomenon brought about by ever expanding building projects, especially the construction of the motorway system, has led to snatched-at evidence, and even produced previously unknown Romano-British town sites. In all this work numismatics has been more and more in evidence as the handmaid of archaeology. Closer assessment of the evidence of coin finds from archaeological sites has led to fresh interpretations of the use of areas of the site, and indications of the changing economic situation, based on analysis of coin losses by denomination at different periods. The lead in this latter approach has been taken by Dr Richard Reece of the Institute of Archaeology of London University. Another worker in the field combining archaeology and numismatics is P. J. Casey of the University of Durham who has been concerned with the re-excavation of selected areas of a number of sites to answer various questions, especially those relating to the latter end of the Roman occupation. Allied to this he has examined in detail and published the coins from a number of earlier excavations and older collections, making in the process some important new finds as well as being able to re-interpret the evidence in many instances in relation to the archaeological record.

In the area of detailed numismatic analysis invaluable research has been carried out by Dr Philip V. Hill on the undated coins of Rome, and especially on those of the Severan series. Whilst concerned with the whole issues of the Roman mint at large such pioneer study has ramifications for Roman Britain in those many types referring to the Province which can now be placed in a stricter chronological framework. Far closer order of the dating of the issues within individual mints of the later Empire has been achieved by Carson, Hill and Kent in their *Late Roman Bronze Coinage*, an essential tool for anyone working on the coins of this period.

With the coins themselves, there have been a number of major finds, particularly of two hoards of gold coins—a very rare occurrence in Britain. A hoard of early imperial aurei was found at Bredgar in Kent in 1957 which had probably been concealed soon after the Roman invasion in A.D. 43. From Water Newton, Cambridgeshire, in February 1974 came a hoard of thirty gold solidi of the House of Constantine, found in a pottery bowl that held a bronze bowl in which were the coins and two pieces of folded silver plate. Numerous hoards of silver and base-metal coins have been retrieved in recent years (many of them being found by the use of metal detectors), of which that from Mildenhall (ancient *Cunetio*), near Marlborough, Wiltshire, comprising some 56,500 coins is the largest hoard of its type yet found in Britain. It has been calculated that it could represent the pay of 190 legionaries for a year. The site was a small posting station on the road to Bath (*Aquae Sulis*). It need hardly be emphasised that with so much new material being discovered any finds of hoards or individual coins should be reported to the local museum. Irrespective of any legal implications of Treasure Trove being involved, it is of the utmost importance that this information is recorded because no matter how small the find they all form part of the greater picture of our view and knowledge of coins and the use of coins in Roman Britain. Painstaking analysis of mints represented and die links, etc., in hoards, large or small, can reveal much new information on the distribution of coins from mints and on the internal structure and organisation of issues from mints.

Individual coins of new types, or unpublished varieties, continue to appear from time to time and are generally to be found first noticed in the monthly *Coin & Medal Bulletin* and *Numismatic Circular*. Of particular interest is an unpublished aureus of Carausius with as obverse an unusual bust, cuirassed and draped left, wearing an ornate crested helmet, and the legend VIRTVS CARAVSI. The style is very like that of the helmeted bust aurei of Postumus, and the piece is almost certainly from early in the reign. The reverse has a standing figure of Sol, left, and the legend ORIES (*sic*) AVG (*see Coin & Medal Bulletin*, 1978, 36–7). Also of special numismatic importance relating to Carausius, the usurper emperor in Britain A.D. 287–293, are the two unique medallions that have appeared, both apparently struck early in his reign. The first is briefly described on p. 34 below (and illustrated here from a drawing by Peter Seaby). The letters in the exergue on the reverse are still a puzzle and, as the piece belongs to the 'unmarked' series, Robert Carson has

suggested that it may have been struck at Boulogne. For long on loan to the British Museum, it was acquired by the Department of Coins and Medals in 1967. A second medallion of Carausius was acquired by the British Museum in 1972. The style of work and the portrait on this piece is better than on the first.

Obverse: IMP C [M A]VR M CARAVSIVS PF AVG GER. Bearded bust of Carausius, left, in consular dress and holding an eagle-tipped sceptre.

Reverse: VICTOR CARAVSIVS AVG GERM MAX. In the exergue: RSR. Carausius, in military dress and helmeted, stands to the left holding a globe in his outstretched right hand and a spear, vertically, in his left. Behind him stands a winged Victory who carries a palm branch in her left hand whilst she crowns the emperor with a laurel wreath held in her right hand.

Although the RSR in the exergue, which also appears on coins of all three metals, has been attributed to Richborough (*Rutupiae*), Carson rules this out on the grounds of the similarity of style between the medallion and denarii with the London mint signature, and therefore assigns it to London. Both medallions are of orichalcum, very similar in their fabric, and their metal was probably obtained from melted down sestertii of previous emperors. It is possible that both medallions came from the same, unrecorded, hoard because, despite having been cleaned before they arrived at the British Museum, they share a similar dark staining. The first medallion was seen in 1931 when it was alleged to come from an old collection in the north of England; the second medallion appeared in a mixed lot of Roman coins from a London street market in 1971. The possibility that the medallions were once associated, and what else might have been with them and may yet appear, is intriguing, as also is Askew's suggestion that the first medallion could have been a 'strike' in base metal from dies intended for a gold medallion—for either of these to appear in gold would place them on a par with the famed gold Arras medallion (p. 54), and amongst the important numismatic 'monuments' of Roman Britain.

In an overall view of the coinage of the Roman Empire the province of Britannia received far more notice on the imperial coins, and on the coins of her usurper emperors, than any of the other provinces. The study of this individual aspect of Roman coinage is one which is interesting, intriguing in the number of still unsolved problems that can be pursued, and very rewarding. To see and examine the coins in their wider context of the Roman Empire and their place and use in the economy and history of the province adds yet another dimension to their intrinsic interest. Gilbert Askew's study of the coins, and his comments on their setting and background history, still opens a window on an aspect of Roman numismatics that is individual and has much to offer to the researcher, student, collector and interested layman alike.

P.A.C.

PREFACE.

Although this book was begun in no light-hearted spirit, but accepted as a serious task from the first, I fear I did not realise the amount of work it would ultimately entail. My intention was to produce something that would primarily interest the numismatist, but would also be worthy of attention by students of Roman Britain. Just how much—or little—success has been achieved must be left to the verdict of my readers, but I wish to make acknowledgement here of the encouragement and assistance I have received from numismatists and archaeologists who read the instalments as they appeared or who were able to help in other ways. Without that encouragement and help the work would have been much worse done, and whatever value the book may have considerably reduced.

First I would offer my grateful thanks to Professor Ian A. Richmond, of King's College, Newcastle-upon-Tyne, who found time in his already overcrowded days to read much of the earlier historical sections, and who offered amendments and additions which have been very willingly incorporated. Thanks no less sincere are due to Lieut.-Col. Eric Birley for his kindness in contributing the appendix on " The Roman Governors of Britain," probably the most valuable section of the whole book. The information it contains would not be accessible elsewhere without a very great deal of scholarship and research.

My best thanks are also due to Mr. Allan P. Pallett, who did a very large share of the work on the Constantinian coinage ; to the staff of the Coin Room of the British Museum for facilities in working through the London coins of the Tetrarchy ; to Dr. J. Grafton Milne, of the Ashmolean Museum, for allowing me access to coins of the same series in the Oxford collection ; to Mr. Colin M. Kraay, also of the Ashmolean Museum, for information about other coins in the Oxford cabinets ; and to Mr. Brian Grover, Mr. Harold Mattingly, Mr. L. G. P. Messenger, Col. G. B. Pears, and Mr. A. M. Woodward, to all of whom I am indebted for constructive help and criticism.

Finally, I should like to record the assistance rendered by the late Mr. R. Cyril Lockett, who allowed me to look through the Romano-British coins in his cabinet and make notes of outstanding rarities : it is a matter of great regret to me that he has not lived to see his kindness duly acknowledged.

GILBERT ASKEW.

Gilbert Askew went into hospital a few days after this book was sent to the printers in its final form. A few days later he passed away. His death is a great loss to numismatics as he was a fine student whose heart and soul was in his work. My staff and I have had to do the final proofing and must take the blame for any errors. We have also had to make the index. Some additions have been kindly supplied by Mr. Pallett, mostly from coins that were in the L. A. Lawrence collection.

This work is, I feel, a worthy memorial to Gilbert Askew and will keep his name alive in numismatic circles.

H. A. SEABY.

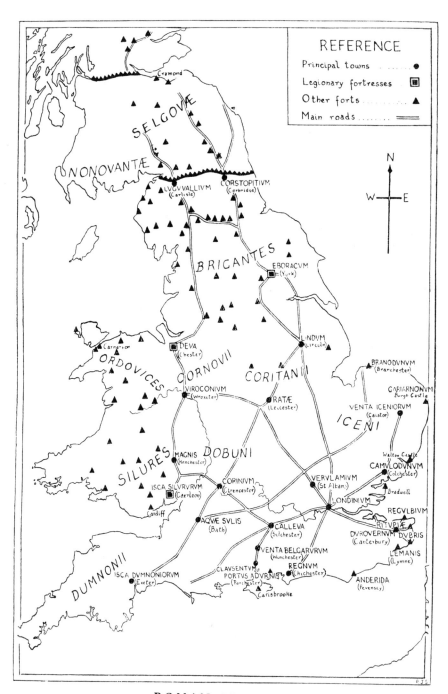

ROMAN BRITAIN

THE COINAGE OF ROMAN BRITAIN

Introduction.

It is little more than a hundred years since the appearance of the third and standard edition of J. Y. Akerman's " Coins of the Romans relating to Britain," and in that period the most far-reaching changes have taken place in the habits, the government and the life of the people of Britain. Even greater, however, is the advancement of our knowledge and appreciation of the archaeology of our own country ; and with the increase in such knowledge a similar increase in the study and application of numismatics has steadily kept pace. To assess and apportion the credit for this improvement would be extremely difficult, as many students and writers have contributed to it in large or small measure ; but we cannot deny to Akerman a goodly share. The book in question was published at half a guinea, and earned for its author not only the " Prix Numismatique " of the French Institute—so says the publisher's advertisement—but also high commendation from the *Archaeological Journal*, whose reviewer said that the work " should be consulted not merely for these particular coins, but also for facts most valuable to all who are interested in Romano-British history." But before we discuss the book, let us consider the man.

John Yonge Akerman was born in London on the 12th June, 1806. In early life he was secretary to William Cobbett, in 1838 to the Greenwich Railway Company; and afterwards he became secretary to Lord Albert Conyngham (later Lord Londes-borough). In January, 1834, he was elected a Fellow of the Society of Antiquaries of London, and in 1848 was made joint secretary of that body with Sir Henry Ellis. Five years later he became sole secretary, which position he held until 1860, when he was compelled by ill-health to resign it and with it the editorship of " Archaeologia."

In 1836 he started, chiefly at his own expense, the *Numismatic Journal*, the first English periodical of its kind. He helped to found the Numismatic Society, which held its first meeting on December 22nd, 1836. He was secretary from that date until 1860 and also editor of the *Numismatic Chronicle*, the society's journal, until the same year. After 1860, Akerman lived at Abingdon until his death on November 18th, 1873.

The bibliography of his published writings given in *Proceedings of the Numismatic Society for* 1874 (in *Num. Chron.*, Vol. XIV, new series, pp. 16 ff.), shows how prolific Akerman was as an author, the most notable of his contributions to numismatic literature being the following :—

" Numismatic Manual," London 1832 and 1840.
" Introduction to the Study of Ancient and Modern Coins," London 1848.
" Descriptive Catalogue of Rare and Unedited Roman Coins," 2 vols., London, 1834.
" Coins of the Romans relating to Britain," 1836, 1842 and 1844.
" Ancient Coins of Cities and Princes," London, 1846.
" Numismatic Illustrations of the New Testament," London, 1846.

He was awarded the gold medal of the French Institute, and was an honorary member of several learned Societies, including the Royal Academy of St. Petersburg and the Instituto di Corrispondenza Archeologica of Rome.

The *Dictionary of National Biography*, from which most of the above particulars are taken, makes no mention of Akerman's education, but that he was something of a scholar is evident from the quotations from classical authors in foot-notes to his " Coins of the Romans relating to Britain " ; and, indeed, he seems also to have studied the best numismatic and archaeological works then available. In this connection we ought to remember that the chief reference books on numismatics which are now in regular use were all written later than 1844. The second edition of Cohen's " Description Historique des Monnaies frappées sous l'empire romain " did not begin appearing until 1880, the last volume being published in 1892, and this work has so long been the standby of students of the Roman coinage that it is difficult to imagine the numismatic world being without it. Akerman had to manage as best he could with Eckhel, Vaillant and similar authors whom the modern student seldom thinks of consulting, although a knowledge of these earlier works is still useful. That Akerman could have done what he did, with only such authorities to aid him, is the best testimony to the value of his work ; and that that value has always been recognised is proved by the continual popularity of his books.

Not that the book under discussion is entirely above criticism in the light of more recent knowledge. It suffers from the defects of its period in that it abounds in moral reflections which seem to our eyes to be out of place in a scientific treatise. Many of Akerman's comments on the various emperors and their coins are coloured by the moral standards of his own time oblivious of the fact that those of the early Roman Empire were somewhat different ; and he is not above using a quotation from Tacitus' " Life of Agricola " in reference to the state of Britain in the late third century, regardless of the effect that two hundred years of Roman rule must have had on the population of the island. Again he discourses learnedly on Britannicus, who had no connection with Britain other than by his name, and describes in detail three coins of that prince which do not relate to Britain in any particular. He devotes several pages to the life and coinage of Clodius Albinus, who was certainly Governor of Britain for a time, but whose coins were all struck either at Rome or Lugdunum and include no types with any reference to Britain.

About thirty pages (of a total of 170) are given to " observations " on Roman coin-moulds discovered in England and France ; but he dismisses the " barbarous radiate " issues of the third century and later, a most important series which still awaits complete and detailed study, in a few lines. He was, however, sufficient of both scholar and numismatist correctly to assess, and readily to discount, some of the wilder assertions of Stukeley, who, though an accurate and valuable archaeological observer in the field, was apt to be both fanciful and unreliable as an author. As regards the Constantinian period and the coinage of the last days of Roman rule in Britain, Akerman deals with these but briefly, and it was left to Jules Maurice (in *Num. Chron.*, Series III, Vol. XX) fully to chronicle the operations of the London mint in the fourth century.

Let it not be thought that the above criticisms of Akerman's book are offered in any carping or hyper-critical spirit, for the present author is all too conscious of his own shortcomings to dream of decrying one who may be counted amongst the great men of English numismatics. Akerman's work is for the most part as sound and reliable as it was when written, and his name will always be remembered in connection with the archaeology and numismatics of Roman Britain.

Having discussed Akerman and his book, the purpose of the present work may be briefly set out. It is an endeavour to provide a catalogue of the principal coins issued by the Romans relating to their British campaigns and victories and of coins struck at mints in the island during the Roman occupation, with some slight outlines of the occupation itself as a back-ground. It is hoped that the coinage of Carausius and Allectus has been dealt with in sufficient detail : all who know this series will realise that any attempt at a *corpus* of the coinage of the first British empire would require a large volume and, perhaps, not be complete even than, as many " unpublished " pieces are known to exist. The " barbarous " issues of the occupation, again, could only be dealt with in detail in a much more comprehensive study, but the attempt has been made to present them as intelligible parts of the whole without discussion in detail. The reader who wishes to make further study of the unofficial coinages will find guidance in the bibliography which appears in Chapter XI.

The phrase used above " relating to their British campaigns and victories " has been interpreted in its strictest sense and not in its widest. For instance, any coin with an obverse legend containing the abbreviation BRIT could be taken as referring to Britain even though the reverse might have some quite different application, e.g., the denarius of Severus with *obv.* SEVERVS PIVS AVG BRIT and *rev.* FELICITAS PVBLICA, Felicitas standing l. holding caduceus and cornucopiae. (*M. & S.* 331). The coinage of Commodus, also, contains a long series of pieces, from 184 to 191 A.D., where the title BRIT forms part of the obverse legend, but only a very small proportion of the reverse legends or types of these can have any reference to Britain. On the other hand, certain coins of Severus and Caracalla bear reverse types which probably refer to operations in Britain, such as that showing a bridge (Severus, *C.* 521 and Caracalla, *C.* 603), or depiction of the emperor on horseback attacking an enemy (Severus, *C.* 536), or the emperor, holding Victory and spear, being crowned by Virtus (Severus, *C.* 538). In the present work, however, only coins with a direct and unmistakable allusion to Britain have been included : coins struck in Britain are, of course, given places regardless of their reverse types or legends.

———— : : ————

Chapter I : Julius Caesar to Hadrian.

One of the best-remembered dates in British history is 55 B.C., the year in which C. Julius Caesar first landed in our island. His reasons for the invasion were essentially military, as Britain was believed to be giving help to the rebellious Gauls ; and, indeed, there was a strong racial link between the Belgic tribes of North Gaul and the Belgic conquerors of Southern Britain. Caesar's first descent on Britain was no more than a reconnaissance in force : his second attack, in the following year, was probably, judging from the much larger number of troops employed, an attempt at conquest. But the second expedition was little more successful than the first, and Caesar withdrew from the island after a stay of a few weeks. He returned to Gaul with hostages from certain of the British tribes, and a promise of tribute which was probably never fulfilled. No doubt that previous to Caesar's visits to Britain there had been some infiltration of Roman coins into the island in the ordinary course of trade, but it is probable that from 54 B.C. onwards the flow of such coinage was increased until the Roman issues were circulating alongside the native currency to which Caesar refers.

Augustus, despite the prophetic note sounded in two of Horace's *Odes* (Book I, 35, and Book III, 5) made no attempt to carry the northern frontier of his empire beyond the coast of Gaul. Tiberius adopted the same conservative policy, and the unbalanced Caligula could do no more than march his legions to the shore of the Channel and bring them back again with the " spoils of the ocean "—sea-shells— as evidence of their prowess. Claudius, however, actuated by a desire to prove himself a true " Imperator," decided to intervene in British affairs and restore the prestige of Roman arms. Accordingly in 43 A.D. he sent his general Aulus Plautius with an army which included four legions (II Augusta, IX Hispana, XIV Gemina and XX Valeria Victrix) with their auxiliaries to conquer the island ; and he himself followed to observe the progress of the campaign. The expedition was well planned and ably led, and operations were carried on methodically and successfully until by 47 the Romans controlled all the country to the south of the Fosse Way, the great road running from Axminster to Lincoln, along which a chain of forts was planted.

About this time the first Roman coins bearing any reference to Britain were struck by order of Claudius :—

1. TI . CLAVD . CAESAR . AVG . P . M . TR . P VI IMP X . Laureate head r.
   R. DE BRITANN on architrave of triumphal arch which is surmounted by equestran statue l., between two trophies.
   N *aureus*, mint of *Rome*, 46-7 A.D. *M. & S.* 8. *B.M.C.* 29.

The arch which forms the reverse type is that which was erected in Rome in 44 A.D. in recognition of the emperor's personal share in the British campaign.

This issue was followed by others bearing the same reverse type, but with different dates in the obverse legend :—

2. TI . CLAVD . CAESAR . AVG . P . M . TR . P . VI IMP XI . Laureate head r.
   R. as preceding.
   N *aureus*, mint of *Rome*, 46-7 A.D. *Cohen* 17. *M. & S.* 9. *B.M.C.* 32-4.

3. *Obv.* and *rev.* as preceding :
   R *denarius*, 46-7 A.D. *C.* 18. *M. & S.* 9. *B.M.C.* 35.

4. As preceding, but *obv.* legend ends TR . P . VIIII . IMP . XVI.
N aureus, 49-50 A.D. *M. & S.* 10. *B.M.C.* 49.

5. As preceding :
R denarius, 49-50 A.D. *C.* 19. *M. & S.* 10. *B.M.C.* 50.

6. As preceding, but *obv.* legend ends TR . P. . VIIII . IMP . XVII.
R denarius, 50-51 A.D. *C.* 20. *M. & S.* 11.

7. As preceding, but *obv.* legend ends XVIII.
R denarius, 50-51 A.D. *C.* 21. *M. & S.* 12.

8. As preceding, but *obv.* legend ends TR . P . X . IMP . P . P .
R denarius, 50-51 A.D. *C.* 22. *M. & S.* 13.

9. As preceding, with TR . P . X . P . P . IMP . XVIII.
N aureus, 50-51 A.D. *C.* 23. *M. & S.* 14.

10. As preceding, with TR . P . XI . IMP . P . P . COS . V.
R denarius, 51-2 A.D. *C.* 24. *M. & S.* 15.

All the foregoing coins were struck in Rome ; but the mint of Caesarea in Cappadocia also issued the following :—

11. TI . CLAVD . CAESAR . AVG . GERM . P . M . TR . P . Laureate head l.

R. Claudius in triumphal quadriga r., holding eagle-tipped sceptre in l. hand. In ex., DE BRITANNIS.

R didrachm. Undated, but probably issued about 46 A.D. *C.* 15. *M.* & *S.* 56. *B.M.C.* 237-9.

No bronze or copper coins were struck by Claudius with any legend relating to Britain, but many of his *asses*, as well as some *sestertii* and *dupondii*, were imitated by unofficial mints in the island. These pieces have been the subject of a special study by Dr. C. H. V. Sutherland,* who has classified them into four grades of increasing degrees of barbarousness. It is considered that the best copies, Grade I, are mostly contemporary ; but Claudian copies are found in hoards that must have been deposited in the second and third centuries, and it is not always certain whether their continuance in circulation can account for this, or whether the types remained in favour and were copied until a comparatively late date.

---

* "Romano-British Imitations of Bronze Coins of Claudius I." American Numismatic Society's Notes & Monographs no. 65, 1935.

The Claudian coins forming the prototypes of these " barbarous imitation:
may be briefly summarised :—

Sestertii.	℞.	SPES AVGVSTA S C
	℞.	EX S C OB CIVES SERVATOS
Dupondii.	℞.	CERES AVGVSTA S C
	Obv.	ANTONIA AVGVSTA. ℞. TI CLAVDIVS CAESAR, etc.
Asses.	℞.	CONSTANTIAE AVGVSTI S C
	℞.	LIBERTAS AVGVSTA S C
	℞.	S C Minerva r., with javelin and shield.

The last-mentioned is by far the commonest of all.   Similar copies of certain Æ
coins of Nero are sometimes found.

Let us now revert to the history of the conquest.   In 47 A.D. P. Ostorius Scapula
compelled the Iceni and East Anglia to submit to him, and then began the reduction
of Wales ; but the hardy tribes of that mountainous country were difficult to deal
with, and about thirty years of campaigning were needed to complete their defeat.
Ostorius began by attacking the tribes of North-East Wales and then turned his
arms against the Silures of South Wales who were commanded by Caratacus.
The capture of the latter did not dishearten the Welsh, and Suetonius Paulinus was
still campaigning against them when the revolt of the Iceni in 61 A.D., under
Boudicca, broke out, and he had to return to the south to deal with the rebels.

The story of the " British warrior queen " has been so often told that a summary
of it will suffice here.   King Prasutagus of the Iceni, when dying, left half his
property to the emperor in the hope that his daughters might be allowed to remain
in possession of the other half ; but the officers and soldiers sent to take possession
looted his house as though it had been that of a conquered enemy, and submitted
Boudicca and the princesses to insult and ill-treatment.   Accordingly, the Iceni,
enraged at these happenings, rose in revolt, and were joined by the Trinovantes :
the rebels attacked and slew Roman officials and traders wherever they could find
them, and sacked the colony of Camulodunum.

The Ninth Legion, the only large body of Roman troops in eastern Britain,
which was stationed at Lincoln under Petillius Cerealis (a commander who did not
in this emergency display the skill which distinguished some of his later operations),
at once marched out to attack the insurgents.   Superior numbers, however,
triumphed for once over Roman discipline, and the Ninth Legion was practically an-
nihilated ; and Petillius only succeeded in escaping to Lincoln with the survivors of
his cavalry.   The momentary diversion of the rebels, however, allowed Suetonius
time to bring his forces, the Fourteenth Legion and part of the Twentieth, through
hostile country to London.   Arriving there, he decided that the town could not be
held, and evacuated it, accompanied by all Romans who were able to follow him.
Meanwhile the rebels, having destroyed Verulamium (St. Albans) converged on the
hapless town, which they sacked and burnt, killing any Roman who fell into their
hands.

Suetonius continued his retreat, closely followed by Boudicca's hordes, until he
reached a position which could be held against superior numbers.   It is probable
that this was somewhere south of the Thames, but its exact location is uncertain.
However, the position reached, Suetonius turned at bay, and on a hill-side, with
flanks and rear covered by forests, he awaited attack.   The Britons, confident in
their strength, attacked bravely, but here Roman discipline and training could be
exercised to the full, and the dense masses of rebels were held.   Then, after the
Roman javelins had taken heavy toll of them, the order to advance was given and
the Roman line rushed forward.   The Britons wavered and broke, but their own

large numbers and huge wagon-train hindered their flight, and they were slaughtered in droves. The pursuit continued until nightfall, and the rebellion was crushed, Boudicca ending her own life. For its gallant conduct in this campaign the Fourteenth Legion was given the additional title " Martia Victrix."

The process of the conquest of Britain suffered a considerable set-back through Boudicca's rebellion, and many years of careful and conciliatory work were necessary to restore peace to the country behind the Fosse Way frontier line. It was not until the reign of Vespasian, who had himself commanded part of the forces of the Claudian invasion, that the advance could be resumed ; but under three successive governors, Petillius Cerealis (71-4), Julius Frontinus (74-8) and Julius Agricola (78-84), the Roman dominion was gradually extended west and northward. Agricola's work is, perhaps, better known than that of his predecessors because of the account left by his son-in-law Tacitus the historian. He was an able soldier and administrator, and saw the importance of the Tyne-Solway and Forth-Clyde frontier lines, both of which he defended with chains of forts. He penetrated deeply into Caledonia and won a victory at Mons Graupius; but his recall in 84 A.D. prevented him from attempting the complete subjugation of Northern Britain. The garrisons he left in the north, however, managed to maintain themselves until the end of the first century and in some cases later ; but their position became increasingly insecure, and although exact details are lacking it is clear that either in the reign of Trajan (98-117 A.D.) or early in that of his successor Hadrian (117-138 A.D.) a major military disaster overtook the Roman forces in the north. There is literary evidence that the Britons successfully revolted about this time, and it is known that the Ninth Legion, then stationed at York, disappears from history, with certain auxiliary units, during this period, so that Hadrian found it necessary to come to Britain himself to restore the situation. He brought with him the Sixth Legion, Victrix, and other reinforcements, and took the opportunity to plan and initiate the system of frontier works, which we know as Hadrian's Wall, between the Tyne and the Solway. This great barrier, which consists of a continuous wall almost from sea to sea, strengthened in many places by a ditch in front of it and defended by forts, mile-castles and turrets, is served by a system of military roads and has behind it the complex of continuous ditch and mounds we now call the Vallum [see map on page 88]. This is not the place to discuss the archaeological problems of the Wall or Vallum, nor of the relation between the two, and we must, therefore, turn to the coins of Hadrian which commemorate his exploits in Britain :—

12. IMP CAESAR TRAIAN HADRIANVS AVG. Laureate head of Hadrian r.

℞. PONT MAX TR POT COS III S C. In ex., BRITANNIA. Britannia seated facing, foot on pile of stones, resting head on r. hand and holding sceptre in l. ; to r., large shield.

Æ *as*, mint of *Rome*, 119-122 A.D. *Cohen* 197. *M. & S.* 577a. *B.M.C.* 1174.

13. As preceding, but with drapery on Hadrian's left shoulder. *M. & S.* 577b. *B.M.C.* 1175.

14.   HADRIANVS AVG COS III P P.   Laur. head r.
R.   BRITANNIA S C.   Britannia seated facing, resting head on r. arm and
holding spear in l., r. foot on pile of stones ; to r., large round shield.
Æ *sestertius*, mint of *Rome*, 134-138 A.D.   *Cohen* 194.   *M. & S.* 845.
B.M.C. 1723.

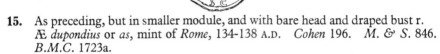

15.   As preceding, but in smaller module, and with bare head and draped bust r.
Æ *dupondius* or *as*, mint of *Rome*, 134-138 A.D.   *Cohen* 196.   *M. & S.* 846.
B.M.C. 1723a.

16.   As preceding, but with laureate and draped bust r.
Æ *dupondius* or *as*, mint of *Rome*, 134-138 A.D.   *Cohen* 195.   *M. & S.* 846.
B.M.C. 1724.

The pile of stones beneath Britannia's right foot, on the reverses of Nos. 12-16,
has been conjectured by some students to allude to Hadrian's wall.

17.   HADRIANVS AVG COS III P P.   Laur. and dr. bust r.
R.   ADVENTVI AVG BRITANNIAE S C.   Emperor, togate, standing r., facing
female figure standing l. and sacrificing with patera over altar ;   beside her,
uncertain animal (? bull).
Æ *sestertius*, mint of *Rome*, 134-135 A.D.   *Cohen* 28.   *M. & S.* 882.   *B.M.C.*,
Vol. III, p. 490.

18. HADRIANVS AVG COS III P P. Bare head cuirassed bust, r.

℞. EXER . BRITANNICVS S C. Emperor on horseback r., raising r. hand, addressing five soldiers, the first of whom holds vexillum and the next three standards. *Illustrated at bottom of page 10.*

Æ *sestertius*, mint of *Rome*, 134-138 A.D. *Cohen* 556. *M. & S.* 912. *B.M.C.* 1672.

19. HADRIANVS AVG COS III P P. Bare head r.

℞. EXERC BRITAN S C in ex. Emperor standing r. on tribunal, raising r. hand, addressing three soldiers, who hold respectively a legionary eagle, a vexillum and shield, and a standard.

Æ *sestertius*, mint of *Rome*, 134-138 A.D. *Cohen* 555. *M. & S.* 913. *B.M.C.* 1672.

The reverse legends of both the above coins are somewhat uncertain, as the only recorded specimens are in poor condition. The illustration is probably composite.

Hadrian arrived in Britain about 122 A.D., but the duration of his stay here is not known. The works he carried out, however, ensured the safety of the northern part of the province for about twenty years.

It will at this point be proper to mention an interesting find made at Verulamium. During the excavations carried out in the Roman city in 1930 and the following years, a Roman coin-die was found in the north-eastern tower of the South-East Gateway, in a deposit which could be dated to the second half of the second century. This coin-die, which is considered to be an official production and not to be connected with any kind of barbarous imitation, is the only example ever found in Britain and is thus of considerable interest. It is of hard bronze, and bears a reverse type of the emperor Hadrian's gold or silver coinage : the legend is ADVENTVS AVG, and the type shows Roma, helmeted and holding spear, greeting the Emperor. (*Cohen* 84. *M. & S.* 225). Its occurrence in Verulamium cannot be explained, as it can have no relation to Hadrian's visit to Britain if the date assigned to this particular reverse, 134-138 A.D., is correct. Had the type been assignable to the coinage of 119-122 A.D. one might have postulated a " travelling mint," part of the emperor's entourage, but this seems to be improbable.

The illustration is reproduced from the report of the Verulamium excavations, by kind permission of the Society of Antiquaries of London.

Chapter II : Antoninus Pius to Commodus.

Despite the military skill lavished upon the Hadrianic barrier system, and the strength of the garrison manning it, the tribes to the north of it continued to give trouble, and about 140 A.D. it became necessary for the Romans to take additional measures for the safety of the northern province. A new barrier was, therefore, constructed between the Forth and the Clyde, somewhat less elaborate than Hadrian's work. On the line first fortified by Agricola a chain of nineteen forts was built, in some cases overlying the Agricolan posts, and the connecting barrier was a wall of turf defended by a larger ditch than that of Hadrian. The date of the construction of this work was 139-142 A.D., under Lollius Urbicus, and the new line was garrisoned by units brought from other parts of Britain. Some came from Hadrian's Wall, which was temporarily abandoned [see map on page 88].

Sufficient military success was obtained against the troublesome natives to justify, in the opinion of the authorities, a new series of coins :—

20. ANTONINVS AVG PIVS P P TR P COS III. Laureate head of Antoninus r.

R̵. IMPERATOR II BRITAN. Victory standing l. on globe, holding wreath and palm.

N̶ aureus, mint of *Rome,* about 143-144 A.D.   *Cohen* 113.   *M. & S.* 113. *B.M.C.,* p. 71.

21. ANTONINVS AVG PIVS P P TR P COS III. Laureate head r., sometimes with drapery on l. shoulder.

R̵. BRITANNIA S C. Britannia, bareheaded, seated l. on rock, holding standard in r. hand and (sometimes) spear against l. arm, l. elbow resting on shield set on helmet.

Æ sestertius, mint of *Rome,* 140-144 A.D.   *Cohen* 116.   *M. & S.* 742. *B.M.C.* 1637.

22. *Obv.* as preceding.

℞. IMPERATOR II around, BRITAN S C in field. Britannia, helmeted, seated l., r. foot on rock, holding spear and resting l. arm on fluted shield with spike. *Illustrated at bottom of page 12.*

Æ *sestertius*, mint of *Rome*, 143-144 A.D. *Cf. Cohen* 115. *M. & S.* 743. *B.M.C.*, p. 264.

23. *Obv.* as preceding.

℞. IMPERATOR II around, BRITAN in ex., S C in field. Britannia, bare-headed seated l. on globe, holding standard in r. hand and spear against l. arm, left elbow resting on shield set on the globe ; below globe, waves.

Æ *sestertius*, mint of *Rome*, 143-144 A.D. *Cohen—. M. & S.* 744. *B.M.C.* 1640.

24. *Obv.* as preceding.

℞. IMPERATOR II around, BRITANNIA in ex., S C in field. Britannia seated l. on rock, holding standard and spear, l. elbow on shield which rests on helmet.

Æ *sestertius*, mint of *Rome*, 143-144 A.D. *Cohen* 119. *M. & S.* 745. *B.M.C.*, p. 264.

25. *Obv.* as preceding.

℞. IMPERATOR II BRITAN S C. Victory standing l. on globe, holding wreath and palm.

Æ *sestertius*, mint of *Rome*, 143-144 A.D. *Cohen* 114. *M. & S.* 719, *B.M.C.* 1613.

26. *Obv.* as preceding.

℞. IMPERATOR II S C. Victory advancing l., holding shield inscribed BRI TAN.

Æ *as*, mint of *Rome*, 143-144 A.D. *Cohen* 442. *M. & S.* 732. *B.M.C.* 1623.

For some ten years there was comparative peace in the north, but in or about 155 A.D. the Brigantes once more rose in revolt, and the Romans had to take the field against them. The victories then gained were commemorated by the following coins :—

27. ANTONINVS AVG PIVS P P TR P XVIII. Radiate head r., sometimes with drapery on l. shoulder.

℞. BRITANNIA COS IIII S C. Britannia seated l. on rock, resting her head on r. hand, l. hand on rock ; to l., round shield and standard.

Æ *dupondius*, mint of *Rome*, 154-155 A.D. *Cohen* 118. *M. & S.* 930. *B.M.C.* 1965.

28. ANTONINVS AVG PIVS P P TR P XVIII. Laur. head r.

℞. Similar to preceding.

Æ *as*, mint of *Rome*, 154-155 A.D. *Cohen* 117. *M. & S.* 934. *B.M.C.* 1971.

This coin is the commonest of all the " Britannia " issues of Antoninus Pius, and although usually allocated to the mint of Rome there is a possibility that the type may also have been struck in this country by a temporary or travelling mint. Certainly this coin is never as well struck as the others, and any specimen classifiable other than " fine " is really rare. The workmanship is always noticeably below standard, for although the dies are in good style the pieces struck from them are frequently on irregular flans and badly centred. That the " Britannia " *as* is common in Britain is proved by many finds, particularly the great votive deposit in Coventina's Well at Carrawburgh on Hadrian's Wall. From this well between 15,000 and 20,000 coins were taken, and of 2,829 of the reign of Antoninus Pius no fewer than 327 were of the type under discussion, a very high proportion.

Although peace was restored to Northern Britain about 158 A.D., it was of brief duration, and early in the reign of Marcus Aurelius the trouble began again—

if, indeed, it had ever properly ceased—and the Romans had once more to deal with the rebellious northern tribes. There are no coins of the joint reigns of M. Aurelius and L. Verus that bear any VICT BRIT types or legends, but the following piece may have reference to the British campaign of that period:—

a   b

29. ANTONIVS AVGVR III VIR R P C. Praetorian galley l.

℞. LEG VI (across field) ANTONINVS ET VERVS AVG REST. Legionary eagle between two standards.

Æ *denarius.* M. & S. 443. B.M.C. 500/1. *Cohen,* M. Antony, 83*.

This coin is, of course, a " restitution " of one of the legionary series of M. Antony, i.e., that struck in honour of his Sixth Legion. The reason for the restitution is not certain, but Mattingly (in *B.M.C.,* Vol. IV, p. cxxiii) suggests that it may have been in honour of Leg. VI. Ferrata for its services in the Parthian war. The issue is confused by there being two Legions numbered VI, " Victrix " (which was in Britain in Hadrian's reign, having been brought from Lower Germany) and " Ferrata " (for many years stationed in Syria and, later, Judaea). H. M. D. Parker, in " The Roman Legions " (*Oxford,* 1928), refers to the two as follows:—

> " By their *cognomina* ' Iron ' and ' Victorious ' both these legions may date back originally to Caesar's sixth legion. This legion was greatly depleted in numbers in the Alexandrine War, and on its arrival in Italy was only 1000 strong. It was, however, brought up to strength and fought at Munda. If it is the source of both the later legions numbered VI, then either it must have been divided after Caesar's death, or one of the two later legions is the direct descendant of Caesar's legion and the other is only Caesarian in the sense that it contained a nucleus of Caesar's *evocati.* The second solution is, I think, more probable. VI Ferrata was probably part of Antony's army . . . and if ἕκτη Μακεδονική mentioned in an inscription from Ephesus . . . is identical with it, then it will have fought at Philippi as one of Antony's eight veteran legions . . . VI Victrix, on the other hand, has the bull emblem and fought for Octavian at Perusia. Possibly, then, VI Ferrata is to be identified with Legion VI which fought at Munda, and VI Victrix was formed by Octavian with a kernel of *evocati,* drawn, perhaps, from the 1000 soldiers who composed Legion VI on its return to Italy from the East."

Although the origin of the two sixth legions may be in doubt, the coin itself answers the question as to whom the issue was intended to honour. Examination of surviving specimens shows that this denarius occurs with two varieties of reverse. No. 29a, above, will be seen to have one of the military standards which flank the legionary eagle surmounted by a figure of Victory. The corresponding standard on 29b is of ordinary type. We may confidently assume, therefore, that 29a refers to Leg. VI. Victrix, and 29b to Leg. VI. Ferrata. The latter legion, no doubt, did good service in the Parthian war, but the authorities of the Imperial mint must have been fully informed regarding the fighting in Northern Britain in which " Victrix " would be frequently and heavily engaged, and care was taken to see that that much-enduring regiment also had a share of the distinction conferred by this commemorative issue.

---

* The illustration is incorrect in that the letters LEG should be between the standard and the legionary eagle.

It is not known how long the first troubles in Aurelius' reign lasted, but it seems that in 169 war broke out again, and that in 175 substantial cavalry reinforcements were sent to Britain ; but soon after the succession of Commodus in March 180, there was an invasion of the province by the tribes of Central Scotland, who over-ran the Antonine Wall and invaded the Lowlands. Of this invasion the authors of " Roman Britain and the English Settlements " say " It was a critical moment in the history of the British frontier, not only as the gravest blow it had ever yet suffered since its first definite organisation by Hadrian, but as the death-knell of an age. Hitherto the initiative had lain with Rome. Henceforth it lay with her enemies. The barbarians were never again to forget the triumphs and the plunder that awaited them beyond those barriers."

Historical sources do not give us the certain date of this Scottish invasion, and the archaeological evidence as to its effects is capable of a variety of interpretations ; but by 184 the situation had been dealt with to sufficient extent to warrant the issue of the following coins :—

30. M COMMODVS ANTONINVS AVG ·PIVS.　Laureate head of Commodus r.

R. P M TR P VIIII IMP VII COS IIII P P S C : in ex., BRITT.　Britannia standing l., holding curved sword and wreath (or patera).

Æ *sestertius*, mint of *Rome*, 184 A.D.　*Cohen* 35.　*M. & S.* 437.　*B.M.C.*, p. 796.

31. M COMMODVS ANTON AVG PIVS BRIT.　Laureate head r.

R. as preceding.

Æ *sestertius*, mint of *Rome*, 184 A.D.　*Cohen* 36.　*M. & S.* 437.　*B.M.C.*—.

32. *Obv.* as preceding.

R. P M TR P VIIII IMP VII COS IIII P P S C : in ex., VICT BRIT.　Victory seated r., about to inscribe shield which she supports on her knee.

Æ *sestertius*, mint of *Rome*, 184-5 A.D.　*Cohen* 945.　*M. & S.* 440.　*B.M.C.* 550-1.

33. *Obv.* as preceding.

R. as preceding except for TR P X instead of TR P VIIII.

Æ *sestertius*, mint of *Rome*, 184-5 A.D.　*Cohen* 946.　*M. & S.* 452.　*B.M.C.* 560.

34. *Obv.* as preceding.

R. as preceding, except for VIC BRIT in exergue instead of VICT BRIT.

Æ *sestertius*, mint of *Rome*, 184-5 A.D.　*Cohen*—.　*M. & S.* 451.　*B.M.C.* 559.

Two large Æ medallions were also struck to record the Roman victories of this campaign :—

35. M COMMODVS ANTONINVS AVG PIVS BRIT. Bust of emperor, laureate, r., wearing paludamentum and cuirass.

℞. BRITTANIA P M TR P X IMP VII COS IIII P P. Britannia, wearing short tunic, mantle and braccae, seated l. on rock : she holds standard with r. hand and spear in l., resting l. arm on oval shield, with central spike and beaded border, which rests on helmet r.

Æ *medallion*, 1.65 in. diameter. *Grueber*, " Roman Medallions in the British Museum," p. 23, No. 12.

36. *Obv.* as preceding.

℞. P M TR P X IMP VII COS IIII. Victory seated r. in cuirass, holding palm in r. hand and supporting with her l. shield resting on her l. knee and inscribed VICT BRIT ; before her, trophy ; behind, shield.

Æ *medallion*, 1.5 in. diameter. *Grueber*, *op. cit.*, p. 24, No. 16.

Although the victories commemorated by these coins and medallions relieved the situation, it seems that the Romans realised that the Antonine Wall could no longer be considered a sufficiently strong obstacle to further invasions, and after a certain amount of reconstruction had been done to it it was deliberately dismantled and abandoned, probably not later than 196, the garrisons withdrawing to strengthen the much more defensible Hadrianic line, which was henceforward the northern frontier of the province.

Chapter III : Clodius Albinus to Geta.

The assassination of Commodus in 192 was the cause of a period of disturbance within the Empire that had a drastic effect on Roman Britain. The situation created was not unlike that at the death of Nero, when the armies in the different provinces elected their own particular commanders to the vacant throne, and civil war was the result. The immediate successor of Commodus was P. Helvius Pertinax, who had held a command in Britain and was popular with the troops. He was hailed Augustus by the praetorian guard, but lost their favour through an attempt to institute certain reforms, and he was soon murdered by those who had at first supported him. The guard then auctioned the purple to the highest bidder, M. Didius Julianus, whose tenure of the imperial power lasted about three months : he was deposed and killed during the advance on Rome of L. Septimius Severus. The latter, who was of African birth, commanded the Pannonian legions, and before coming to Rome he had defeated Pescennius Niger, the nominee of the Syrian army. He had conciliated Clodius Albinus, who had the support of the legions of Britain and Gaul, by appointing him his successor with the rank of Caesar ; but once safely in Rome, with Julianus and Niger both out of the way, he turned against the man he had favoured. Severus caused Albinus to be declared a public enemy, and Albinus in return had himself proclaimed emperor, crossed from Britain to Gaul with all the troops he could gather, and made Lugdunum his headquarters. In the ensuing struggle the army of Albinus was defeated, and its commander committed suicide. Thus Severus was left sole master of the Roman world in 197 A.D.

The effect on Roman Britain, however, was disastrous and far-reaching. Denuded of most of its defenders, the province was once more the prey of the northern invaders and their Brigantian allies. All over the north there was destruction of Roman buildings : not only did Hadrian's wall undergo damage which amounted in some sections to complete demolition, but even the legionary fortress at York suffered severely. The walled towns of the southern part of the province were secure within their defences, but elsewhere the destruction was enormous. Severus, unable then to attend to British affairs in person on account of his eastern expedition, appointed a new Governor, Virius Lupus, under whom the work of reconstruction was begun. By the time Severus arrived in Britain, 208 A.D., the Hadrianic frontier works had been restored, and punitive expeditions against the Scottish tribes planned and begun ; and the victories subsequently gained were referred to in the following coins, Nos. 37 to 55, all of which are from the mint of Rome :—

37. SEVERVS PIVS AVG. Laur. head of Severus r.

R. VICTORIAE BRIT. Victory advancing r., head l., leading captive by hand and carrying trophy.

N aureus. M. & S. 302. *C.* 726. 206-210 A.D.

38. As preceding, but Æ *denarius.*

39. *Obv.* as preceding.

R. VICTORIAE BRIT. Victory, nude to waist, standing facing, head r., holding palm : to r., palm-tree with shield attached.

Æ *denarius. M. & S.* 302A. 206-210 A.D.

40. SEVERVS PIVS AVG BRIT. Laur. head r.
℟. VICTORIAE BRIT. Victory advancing r., holding wreath and palm.
Æ *denarius. M. & S.* 332. *C.* 727.* 210-211 A.D.

41. As preceding, but Victory standing l.
Æ *denarius. M. & S.* 333. *C.* 728. 210-211 A.D.

42. As preceding, but Victory advancing l.
N *aureus. M. & S.* 334. 210-211 A.D.

43. As preceding, but Victory seated l., about to inscribe shield set on her knee.
Æ *denarius. M. & S.* 335. *C.* 731. 210-211 A.D.

44. As preceding, but Victory standing facing, head r., holding palm and fastening shield to a palm-tree.
Æ *denarius. M. & S.* 336. *C.* 730. 210-211 A.D.

45. As preceding, but shield already attached to palm-tree.
Æ *denarius. M. & S.* 337. *C.* 729. 210-211 A.D.

46. L SEPT SEVERVS PIVS AVG BRIT. Laur. head r.
℟. VICT BRIT P M TRP XIX COS III PP S C. Two Victories standing r. and l., affixing shield to palm-tree, at the foot of which are two captives.
Æ *sestertius. M. & S.* 808. *C.* 723 (no BRIT on *obv*).* 211 A.D.

47. SEVERVS PIVS AVG. Radiate head r.
℟. Legend as preceding : Victory standing r., holding vexillum with both hands : on either side of her, a seated captive.
Æ *dupondius. M. & S.* 809. *C.* 725. 211 A.D.

48. SEVERVS PIVS AVG BRIT. Laur. head r.
℟. As preceding.
Æ *as. M. & S.* 812A. *C.* 724. 211 A.D.

---

* Mr. L. G. P. Messenger's specimen, formerly in the Walters collection, has no BRIT. on obv., the legend being complete without it.

49. As preceding, but with drapery on l. shoulder.
Æ *as.* *M. & S.* 812B. *C.* 724. 211 A.D.

50. L SEPT SEVERVS PIVS AVG. Laur. head r.
℞. VICTORIAE BRITTANNICAE S C. Type as No. 46.
Æ *sestertius.* *M. & S.* 818. *C.* 732. 206-210 A.D.

51. IMP CAE L SEP SEVERVS . . . AVG. Laur. head r.
℞. VICTORIAE BRITTANNICAE S C. Type as No. 47, but Victory holds trophy.
Æ *sestertius.* *M. & S.* 819. *C.* 737. 206-210 A.D.
(This coin is regarded as doubtful, owing to the anomalous obverse).

52. SEVERVS PIVS AVG BRIT. Radiate head r.
℞. VICTORIAE BRITTANNICAE S C. Victory standing r., foot on helmet (or globe) inscribing shield set on palm-tree.
Æ *dupondius.* *M. & S.* 834. *C.* 735. 210-211 A.D.

53. SEVERVS PIVS AVG BRIT. Laur. head r.
℞. Legend as preceding, type as No. 47.
Æ *as.* *M. & S.* 837a. *C.* 736. 210-211 A.D.

54. As preceding, with drapery on l. shoulder.
Æ *as.* *M. & S.* 837b. *C.* 736. 210-211 A.D.

55. SEVERVS PIVS AVG BRIT. Laur. head r.
℞. As No. 52.
Æ *as.* *M. & S.* 837A. *C.* 734. 210-211 A.D.

It is notable that the victories of Severus in Britain were considered of sufficient importance to be the subject of commemorative issues by the mint of Alexandria : it may be that Severus' African birth had something to do with this. A small issue of coins with reverse legend NIKH KATA BPETANNΩN (variously abbreviated) occurs during his reign. The following piece, No. 55a, and a similar coin of Geta, No. 95a, have been recorded, and it is probable that similar tetradrachms were struck for Caracalla.

55a. Legend uncertain, but probably AYT K Λ CEΠ CEYH EYCE ΠEPT CEB APA AΔI, or variant thereof : laur. head r.

℞. NEIKH KATA BPET. Nike flying l. : in field, LIZ. *Billon tetradrachm of Alexandria.* Milne, " Catalogue of Alexandrian Coins in the Ashmolean Museum," No. 2726.

In addition to these coins of official mintage, mention should be made of a small series of " barbarous " *denarii* found by Professor Newstead in excavations on the Deanery Field, Chester, 1924-26. These are considered by Mattingly* to be the products of an irregular mint which may have issued money for the troops. The recorded types are as follows :—

56. L · S · SEVE . . . , Laur. head r.

℞. PAET · MA · · · · MIR P VOI. Aequitas standing l., holding scales and cornucopiae.

57. . . . S . . . SEV · PERT · · · · AVG · IMP · . Laur. head r.

℞. TR · P · VI VI IMP · II COS · IIII. Libertas standing l., holding pileus and cornucopiae.

58. - - - ESPA (?) AVG IMT I. Laur. head r.

℞. FIDES MILITVM. Fides standing l., holding standard in each hand.

These " barbarous " die-struck *denarii* must not be confused with the cast contemporary forgeries which occasionally turn up in Britain. The latter, however, although sometimes exhibiting the types of Severus' reign, are more likely to be of a somewhat later manufacture. The clay moulds for their production have been found on various British sites, and include obverses and reverses of Severus, Caracalla, Geta, Julia Domna, Plautilla and Severus Alexander. Such a mould was found at Housesteads, Northumberland, in 1932, bearing an impression of the obverse of a *denarius* of Julia Domna on one side, IVLIA AVGVSTA, bust r., and the impression of the reverse of a coin of Severus on the other, VICT AVGG COS II P P. Victory l., with wreath and palm (*Severus, Cohen* 694). That the coins made from such moulds circulated along with the regular issues is proved by their being found together on excavated sites : witness the piece found at Risingham, Northumberland, about 1841, which is now in the Black Gate Museum, Newcastle-upon-Tyne.** It reads as follows :—

P SEPT GETA CAES PONT. Bare head, draped bust, r.

℞. P M TR P III COS III P P. Providentia standing l., holding baton and cornucopiae : at her feet, globe ; in field, r. a star.

This cast *denarius* is also of interest as it has been made from an obverse of Geta and a reverse of Elagabalus, showing that it could not have been produced until 220 A.D. or later. Apparently the fabricators did not take much care to see that the moulds were correctly " matched " before pouring in the molten metal.

---

* In *Num. Chron.* Series V., vol XII, 1932. " The Coinage of Septimius Severus and his times : mints and chronology."

** Archaeologia Aeliana. 4th Series. Vol. X. 1933, p. 94.

The sons of Severus, Caracalla and Geta, accompanied their father on his British expedition, and shared with him the series of coins issued to record the success of the campaign. Those of **Caracalla** are as follows, all being of the mint of Rome :—

59. ANTONINVS PIVS AVG. Laur. head of Caracalla r.

℟. VICTORIA BRIT. Victory standing r.

Æ *denarius. M. & S.* 169. *C.* 627. 206-210 A.D.

60. *Obv.* as preceding.

℟. VICTORIAE BRIT. Victory advancing r., dragging captive and holding trophy.

Ν *aureus. M. & S.* 172. *C.* 628. 206-210 A.D.

61. *Obv.* as preceding.

℟. VICTORIAE BRIT. Victory adv. r., holding trophy in both hands.

Æ *denarius. M. & S.* 172A. 206-210 A.D.

62. *Obv.* as preceding.

℟. VICTORIAE BRIT. Victory advancing l., holding wreath and palm.

Æ *denarius. M. & S.* 173. *C.* 631. 206-210 A.D.

63. *Obv.* as preceding.

℟. VICTORIAE BRIT. Victory seated l. on shields, holding shield on her r. knee, and palm.

Ν *aureus. M. & S.* 174. *C.* 633. 206-210 A.D.

64. M AVREL ANTONINVS PIVS AVG. Laur. bust r., with drapery on l. shoulder.

℟. VICTORIAE BRITTANNICAE S C. Victory standing r., l. foot on helmet, erecting trophy : to r., woman, towered, standing facing, and captive seated r.

Æ *sestertius. M. & S.* 464. *C.* 639. 206-210 A.D.

65. *Obv.* legend as preceding : laur. head r.

℞. Legend as preceding : two Victories standing r. and l., setting shield on palm : at foot of palm, two captives seated.

Æ *sestertius. M. & S.* 465a. *C.* 638. 206-210 A.D.

66. As preceding, but *obv.* type laur. bust r., with drapery on l. shoulder.

Æ *sestertius. M. & S.* 465b. 206-210 A.D.

67. ANTONINVS PIVS AVG. Radiate head, r.

℞. VICTORIAE BRITTANNICAE S C. Victory standing r., about to inscribe shield set on palm.

Æ *dupondius. M. & S.* 467. *C.* 637. 206-210 A.D.

68. ANTONINVS PIVS AVG BRIT. Laur. head r.

℞. VICTORIA BRIT. Victory advancing l., holding wreath and palm.

N *quinarius. M. & S.* 230. 210-213 A.D.

69. As preceding, but *rev.* legend VICTORIAE BRIT.

Æ *denarius. M. & S.* 231. *C.* 632. 210-213 A.D.

70. *Obv.* as preceding.

℞. VICTORIAE BRIT. Victory advancing r., carrying trophy in both hands.

Æ *denarius. M. & S.* 231A. *C.* 629. 210-213 A.D.

71. M AVREL ANTONINVS PIVS AVG BRIT. Laur. head l.

℞. VICT BRIT P M TR P XIIII COS III P P S C. Type as No. 64.

Æ *sestertius. M. & S.* 483a. *C.* 641. 211 A.D.

72. As preceding, but *obv.* type laur. bust r., with aegis on l. shoulder.

Æ *sestertius. M. & S.* 483b. *C.* 641. 211 A.D.

73. *Obv.* as No. 71.
℞. As preceding, without P M and P P.
Æ *sestertius.* *M. & S.* 483c. 211 A.D.

74. M AVREL ANTONINVS PIVS AVG. Laur. bust r., with drapery on l. shoulder.
℞. as No. 71.
Æ *sestertius.* *M. & S.* 483d. *C.* 640. 211 A.D.

75. M AVREL ANTONINVS PIVS AVG. Laur. head r.
℞. as No. 71, without P M.
Æ *sestertius.* *M. & S.* 483e. 211 A.D.

76. M AVREL ANTONINVS PIVS AVG BRIT. Laur. bust r., with drapery on l. shoulder.
℞. VICT BRIT P M TR P XIIII COS III P P S C. Victory standing r., l. foot on helmet, inscribing shield set on palm.
Æ *sestertius.* *M. & S.* 484. 211 A.D.

77. ANTONINVS PIVS AVG BRIT. Radiate head r.
℞. VICT BRIT TR P XIIII COS III S C. Type as preceding.
Æ *dupondius.* *M. & S.* 487a. *C.* 644. 211 A.D.

78. ANTONINVS PIVS AVG. Radiate head r.
℞. as preceding.
Æ *dupondius.* *M. & S.* 487b. 211 A.D.

79. ANTONINVS PIVS AVG BRIT. Laur. head r.
℞. as preceding.
Æ *as.* *M. & S.* 490. *C.* 642. 211 A.D.

80. ANTONINVS PIVS AVG BRIT. Radiate head r.
℞. VICTORIAE BRITTANNICAE S C. Victory seated l. on shields, resting shield on knee and holding palm.
Æ *dupondius.* *M. & S.* 516. *C.* 635. 210-213 A.D.

81. *Obv.* as preceding.
℞. VICTORIAE BRITTANNICAE S C. Type as No. 47.
Æ *dupondius. Evans Collection, Ashmolean Museum, Oxford. Not in M. & S. or Cohen.* 210-213 A.D.

82. *Obv.* as preceding, but with laur. head r.
℞. As No. 80, but with BRITANNICAE.
Æ *as.* *M. & S.* 521. *C.* 634. 210-213 A.D.

83. ANTONINVS PIVS AVG BRIT. Laur. head r.
℞. VICTORIAE BRITANICAE S C. Type as No. 76.
Æ *as.* *Cf.* *M. & S.* 522a. *C.* 636. 210-213 A.D.

84. As preceding, with *obv.* type laur. bust r., with drapery on l. shoulder.
Æ *as.* *Cf.* *M. & S.* 522b. *C.* 636. 210-213 A.D.

The coins struck for **Geta** may be summarised as under :—

85. P SEPT GETA PIVS AVG BRIT. Laur. head of Geta r.
R. VICTORIAE BRIT. Victory advancing r., holding wreath and palm.
Æ *denarius. M. & S.* 91. *C.* 220. 210-212 A.D.

86. *Obv.* as preceding.
R. VICTORIAE BRIT. Victory half-nude, standing l., holding wreath and palm.
Æ *denarius. M. & S.* 92. *C.* 219. 210-212 A.D.

86a. IMP CAES P SEPT GETA PIVS AVG. Laur. head r.
R. As No. 85.
Æ *denarius. M. & S.*—. *C.*—. *Not in B.M.C.* 209-210 A.D. *Apparently unpublished.*

87. IMP CAES P SEPT GETA PIVS AVG. Laur. bust r., with aegis on l. shoulder.
R. VICTORIAE BRITTANNICAE S C. Victory seated r. on arms, inscribing shield set on her knee ; behind, shield.
Æ *sestertius. M. & S.* 166. *Cf. C.* 221. 209-210 A.D.

88. *Obv.* as preceding.
R. Legend as preceding : type as No. 65.
Æ *sestertius. M. & S.* 167. *C.* 224. 209-210 A.D.

89. P SEPTIMIVS GETA PIVS AVG BRIT. Laur. head r.
R. VICT BRIT TR P III COS II S C. Victory seated r. on cuirass, inscribing shield set on knee : in front and behind, shields and arms.
Æ *sestertius. M. & S.* 172a. *C.* 210. 211 A.D.

90. As preceding, but *obv.* type laur. bust r., with drapery on l. shoulder.
Æ *sestertius. M. & S.* 172b. *C.* 210. 211 A.D.

91. *Obv.* legend as preceding : bare head r.
R. as preceding.
Æ *as. M. & S.* 178. *C.* 211. 211 A.D.

92. *Obv.* legend as preceding : laur. head r.
R. VICT BRIT TR P IIII COS II S C. Type as preceding.
Æ *sestertius. M. & S.* 180. 212 A.D.

93. *Obv.* as preceding.
R. VICTORIAE BRITTANNICAE S C. Victory standing r., foot on helmet, erecting trophy : to r., Britannia standing facing, hands tied behind back : at her feet, captive.
Æ *sestertius. M. & S.* 186. *C.* 223. 210-212 A.D.

94. *Obv.* as preceding.

℞. Legend as preceding : Victory seated l. on shields, balancing shield on r. knee and holding palm.

Æ *as.* *M. & S.* 191a. 210-212 A.D.

95. *Obv.* legend as preceding : laur. bust r., with drapery on l. shoulder.

℞. as preceding.

Æ *as.* *M. & S.* 192b. 210-212 A.D.

95a. ΑΥΤ Κ ΠΟΥ ϹΕΠ ΓΕΤΑϹ ϹΕΒ or similar : laur. bust r.

℞. ΝΕΙΚΗ ΚΑΤΑ ΒΡΕΤΑΝ. Nike adv. l., with wreath and palm : in field, ΛΙΘ. *Billon tetradrachm of Alexandria.* *B.M.C.* " *Alexandria,*" No. 1481.

From 208 to 211 A.D. Severus conducted campaigns in Scotland ; he carried out extensive building operations at Corbridge (Corstopitum), which he used as a base, and set up a naval station at Cramond on the Forth. His troops pressed far into Scotland, but no great or decisive victory was ever gained over the Caledonian tribes, who always avoided a pitched battle with the legions and instead harassed them by guerrilla attacks. In 211 the emperor, aged and worn out by the rigours of this type of warfare, died at York, and his sons forthwith patched up a peace with the Caledonians and returned to Rome.

Although Severus' campaigns did not entirely destroy the power of the Northern tribes to make trouble in Southern Britain, yet the losses he inflicted on them, and the devastation of their country, had so salutary an effect that the Hadrianic frontier, duly restored, enjoyed unbroken peace for nearly a hundred years afterwards.

Caracalla and Geta, although left by Severus as joint rulers of the Empire, had for years been on the worst of terms with each other, and the savage and jealous nature of Caracalla admitted of no sharing of the purple. In 212 A.D., therefore, he had Geta murdered, and ordered that all statues of the dead man should be destroyed, all inscriptions in his honour erased, and all coins bearing his effigy or titles melted down. Thus the coins of Geta are somewhat rarer than those of Caracalla ; and inscriptions have been found in Britain from which the name of Geta has been removed.

CHAPTER IV : 211-287 A.D.

After the departure of Caracalla and Geta from Britain the province settled down to a period of comparative peace and prosperity. The troops that had been employed in the Caledonian wars returned to their normal stations and carried out such rebuilding and repair of them as was necessary. The hard lessons taught the northern tribes by Severus had been taken to heart, and little trouble came from beyond the Wall ; and Britain's isolated position kept her free from the political disorders and civil commotions that bulk so largely in the history of the Roman Empire in the third century. The succession of the various emperors after the death of Caracalla, and the rise and collapse of the Gallic empire, affected Britain comparatively little. If a usurper controlled Gaul he also controlled Britain, and the British officials seem to have been indifferent as to whether they owed allegiance to the Gallic capital or to Rome. No Governor of Britain thought it worth while to attempt to hold Britain for the central government and, therefore, none of the Gaulish rulers needed to make any expedition to reduce the island. Thus for this period we have no coins dealing with victories in Britain, and the only pieces relating at all to Britain are the following *aurei* of Victorinus, who ruled Gaul and Britain from *c.* 265 to 270 A.D.

96 IMP C VICTORINVS P F AVG. Jugate heads of Victorinus, laureate, and Sol, radiate, l.

℞. LEG XX VAL VICTRIX. Boar at bay l. : in ex., P F.

Ñ aureus. M. & S. 21. *C.* 65.

97 IMP C VICTORINVS P F AVG. Laur. head l.

℞. As preceding.

Ñ aureus. M. & S. 22. *C.* 66.

These two coins form part of the series of " legionary " issues of Victorinus, struck to honour the different legions either composing his forces or those he thought might ultimately give their allegiance to him. Some of the legions thus commemorated were not stationed in territory held by him, and the reason for coins being struck in their honour can only be guessed at ; but the XX Legion, Valeria Victrix, was stationed at Chester and, therefore, under his control. It is possible that coins were also struck for the other two British legions, II at Caerleon and VI at York, but specimens have never yet come to light.

Although Britain at this time was quiet politically, economically she was not so fortunate, and the disturbed state of the continent seems to have had a definite effect on the supply of coinage from the mints of Gaul and Rome : there was, of course, no official Roman mint in the island at this time. The ordinary purposes of trade require a supply of small change to facilitate dealing, apart from the larger coins needed for more important transactions, and when the supply of officially issued coins began to diminish it was supplemented by copies struck in the island from home-made dies. Such dies were often well made, but the craftsmen who produced them seem to have been without much learning or ability to read the Latin language, for although the coin *types* were often well imitated the reproduction of the *legends* is usually less good. Obverse and reverse inscriptions often consist of a mere jumble of letters and in some cases the identification of the original is very difficult.

These " barbarous radiates," as they are generally termed, derive from the base *antoniniani* of the third century, and the coinages of most of the emperors between 258 A.D. and 296 A.D. have been discovered to be copied ; but by far the greater number of copies appears to originate in the issues of Tetricus I and his son Tetricus II who ruled in Gaul about 270-273 A.D.   The official Æ coins of the senior prince are struck from well-made dies, and show his crowned and bearded bust with legend IMP C TETRICVS P F AVG or similar : a common reverse is PAX AVG with a not ungraceful figure of Peace standing holding her olive branch in one hand and a sceptre in the other.   An imitation of this type of coin, however, which the author once saw, depicted the emperor wearing his radiate crown at a very rakish angle, and all that could be read of the obverse legend was PICVS : the reverse showed Peace looking very like a scare-crow, with the letters PAX AG.   This was a " good " imitation, so that the reader can imagine to what depths of grotesqueness the worst copies descend.

Broadly speaking, the better the imitation is, the earlier in the series it should be placed ; for the later imitations suffered in design by being copied not from officially issued coins but from the earlier copies themselves.   The size of the pieces, too, tends to show a gradual reduction, owing to the growing shortage of suitable metal.   To illustrate these two points the author has drawn, from photographs of actual examples, three specimens of increasing barbarity : these three have been chosen because they appear to descend from the same prototype.

G A. del, 1943

Figure A is a fairly good imitation of a coin of Victorinus with reverse of, probably, a " Virtus " type, the figure being Mars, Virtus or a soldier standing holding a spear and resting his left hand on a shield.   Part of the obverse legend can be read ORINVS, and the figure on the reverse is unmistakeable.   Now look at B, which shows no trace of lettering, the dotted border having become a wide circle, and the standing figure a child's scrawl although still recognisable.   C is even worse, there being no border at all and the reverse type crude and meaningless.   Observe, too, the gradual decrease in size, although C does not by any means mark the limit of this reduction.   Some hoards of the smaller pieces or " radiate minimi " as they are termed, have been composed largely of coins only half the size of that shown here, although occasionally of much more careful manufacture.

The dating of these " barbarous radiates " is extremely difficult and has given rise to much controversy.   There are two main schools of thought, one of which holds that these imitations were issued almost contemporaneously with the types copied and that they continued in production until the advent of a later type of official coinage, the Constantinian, offered prototypes for a new series of copies. The other party contends that the " barbarous radiates " represent a coinage issued after the Romans had withdrawn from Britain and the natives thrown upon their own resources.   There are also other theories.   It is not for the present author to offer any solution when wiser men than he have failed to agree, but he suggests that both main theories are, within limits, correct. Certainly imitations of the Tetrician coinage have been found along with official issues in hoards that must have been deposited about 270-275 A.D., and a hoard of very small pieces, smaller, some of them, than that drawn in Figure C, was found during excavations in the Roman theatre of Verulamium, where it must have been concealed before *c.* 300 A.D. On the other hand, some of the largest hoards of the very small pieces have been found in circumstances that suggest a very late date, possibly well into the 5th century A.D. for their deposition.

It is interesting to note that some reverses of " barbarous radiates " appear to be copied from ancient British coins, but this can mean no more than that a few of these early issues were available for use as models when the copies were made.

As has been said above, the political disturbances of the third century had little effect on Britain ; but the island was not entirely to escape the effects of the weakening of Roman power. About the time of the beginning of Diocletian's reign, 284 A.D., the North Sea and the Channel became infested with Frankish and Saxon pirates, and the Roman " Channel Fleet," the *Classis Britannica*, was strengthened in order to deal with the increasing menace of their incursions.

The Romans had maintained a fleet in the Channel from the first century A.D. onwards : its earliest base was probably Boulogne, but later it seems to have had permanent stations at Dover and Lympne. To the command of this fleet Maximianus, the colleague of Diocletian, now appointed a new " admiral," M. Aurelius Mausaeus Carausius, and thus one of the most remarkable personalities in early British history appears on the scene.

Carausius is described by the Roman historians as a citizen of Menapia and of humble extraction. The Menapians were a seafaring and trading people who had their home in what is now Holland, between the Rhine and the Scheldt, but they had also settled at various points on the British and Irish coasts, so that Carausius, although *Menapiae civis*, may have actually been of British birth. A sailor from his boyhood, later a pilot, he became a soldier of eminence under Maximianus, and his military abilities combined with his skill as a seaman caused him to be chosen to command the fleet. A man of the people, and a born leader, he was readily able to secure the loyalty and even, perhaps, the affection of those under his charge, and he very soon saw the strength of his position and the opportunities it offered for enriching himself. The historians say that instead of destroying the pirates he permitted them to make their raids on the coastal towns and villages, and fell upon them when they were returning laden with plunder, much of the latter being kept for himself and not restored to the hapless owners. Some account of these practices reached the ears of Maximianus, who at once ordered the arrest of Carausius ; but the wily seaman, knowing only too well what his fate would be, and believing himself secure in the devotion of his men, turned the tables on the emperor and took his fleet and fighting men to Britain. By means upon which the ancient historians do not agree but which were certainly effective, he won over the British tribes, and rapidly consolidated his position. If the traditional accounts are true, he landed, not on the south coast, but in Westmoreland, having sailed down the Channel and up the Irish Sea. Established in a base ashore, he sent embassies to the Picts and Scots with offers of friendship and asking their assistance in overthrowing the Roman rule : the northern peoples ultimately agreed to help, each with the proviso that any treachery on the part of the other should be prevented. An agreement was reached and the forces of Carausius and his allies marched south. Near York his army encountered the troops of the Roman Governor Quintus Bassianus (otherwise unrecorded as holding that office) and defeated them, owing largely to a British contingent attached to Bassianus' army refusing to take any active part in the struggle. The British levies left the Roman array and withdrew, in formation, to some neighbouring hills, and the Governor's forces, thus deprived of flanking protection, were soon broken, Bassianus and Hirtius the " Procurator Caesaris " being killed on the ensuing rout. Carausius thus destroyed the chief barrier to his conquest of the province, marched on London, and made himself emperor. That his rule extended over the northern areas as well as the south is proved by a milestone[1] found near Carlisle in 1894 which bears the inscription IMP C M AVR MAVS CARAVSIO P F INVICTO AVG. This stone was inverted and re-used under a succeeding emperor, as the other end is inscribed FL VAL CONSTANT—O NOB CAES, referring perhaps to Constantius Chlorus (who restored the island to the central government) or, less probably, to his son Constantine, afterwards the Great.

It should be emphasised that the details of Carausius' landing in Britain and subsequent operations are not available in any contemporary source, but come to us in the works of two Scottish chroniclers, John of Fordun and Hector Boethius, who wrote in the fourteenth and fifteenth centuries respectively, or thereabouts. These and other sources of Carausian history are dealt with at length in Percy H. Webb's " Reign and Coinage of Carausius " (in *Numismatic Chronicle*, 4th series, Vol. VII, 1907, and issued as a separate work by Spink & Son, Ltd., 1908).

Carausius, now master of Britain and part of Northern Gaul, proceeded to establish mints, first at London and later at Colchester. He had, later, another mint at Rouen for a time, and may have also issued coins at Rutupiae (Richborough) but the latter possibility is still in dispute. He struck coins in gold, silver and copper, and the gold is always of good style although somewhat uneven in weight. The silver, comparatively few specimens of which have survived, is also variable in style and quality of metal, but the later pieces are much better in every way than the earlier. It is not possible, within the limits of this essay, to give a complete list of all the known coins, as those recorded in Mattingly and Sydenham, " *Roman Imperial Coinage*," Vol. V, Part 2, number 1097, and many " unpublished " pieces could be added to increase this figure ; but the coinage will be dealt with here on the following scheme. A numbered list of all obverse legends will be given, followed by a series of obverse types, lettered for reference. These will be followed by a table of mint-marks, also numbered for reference. The chief gold and silver coins will then be set out with references to legend, type of bust, and mint-mark ; but the *antoniniani* will be recorded by reverse legends and types only, the barbarous coins with blundered legends being ignored. References to the appropriate volume of M. & S. will be given, as it is from that source that the coin-lists have chiefly been compiled.

❖

---

[1] " Catalogue of Roman Inscribed and Sculptured Stones in the Carlisle Museum. Tullie House," p. 35, No. 94.

Chapter V : The Coinage of Carausius.

Obverse Legends :—

1. IMP C CARAVSIVS P F AVG.
2. IMP C CARAVSIVS P AVG.
3. IMP C CARAVSIVS IVG.
4. IMP C CARAVSIVS AVG.
5. IMP CARAVSIVS P F AVG.
6. IMP CARAVSIVS P F AV.
7. IMP CARAVSIVS P F AVG.
8. IMP CARAVSIVS P AV.
9. IMP CARAVSIVS AVG.
10. IMP C M AVR M CARAVSIVS P AVG.
11. IMP C M AV M CARAVSIVS P F AVG.
12. IMP C M A CARAVSIVS AVG.
13. IMP C M CARAVSIVS P F AVG.
14. IMP C M CARAVSIVS P AVG.
15. IMP C M CARAVSIVS AVG.
16. IMP C CARAVSIVS P F INV or IN or I AVG.
17. IMP C CARAVSIVS IN AVG.
18. IMP C CARAVSIVS PIVS FEL AVG.
19. IMP C CARAVSIVS P F AV.
20. IMP C CARAVSIVS P F AG or AVVG.
21. IMP C CARAVSIVS F AVG.
22. IMP C CARAVSIVS P AV.
23. IMP C CARAVSIVS P IVG.
24. IMP C CARAVSIVS IIG.
25. IMP AVR CARAVSIVS AVG.
26. IMP M CARAVSIVS P AVG.
27. IMP CARAVSIVS P F IN AVG.
28. IMP CARAVSIVS P F I AVG.
29. IMP CARAVSIVS P E or F A AG or AVIG.
30. IMP CARAVSIVS P F IIG.
31. IMP CARAVSIVS P E AVG.
32. IMP CARAVSIVS P E AG.
33. IMP CARAVSIVS P I AVG.
34. IMP CARAVSIVS INIVI.
35. IMP CARAVSIVS INIC.
36. IMP CARAVSIVS P F A.
37. IMP CARAVSIVS P F.
38. IMP CARAVSIVS AV.
39. IMP CARAVSIVS A.
40. IMP CARAVSIVS IVG IIG or II.
41. CARAVSIVS P F AVG.
42. CARAVSIVS AVG.
43. CARAVSIVS ET FRATRES SVI.
44. INVICTO ET CARAVSIO AVG.
45. VIRTVS CARAVSI AVG.
46. VIRTVS CARAVSI A.
47. VIRTVS CARAVSII.
48. VIRTVS CARAVSSI.
49. VIRTVS CARAVSI.
50. VIRT CARAVSI AVG.

Varieties of Obverse Types :—

A. Radiate and draped bust of Carausius r.
AA. Radiate and draped bust l.
B. Laur. and dr. bust r.
BB. Laur. and dr. bust l., holding sceptre.
C. Rad., dr. and cuir. bust r.
D. Laur., dr. and cuir. bust r.
E. Laur. and cuir. bust r.
EE. Laur. and cuir. bust l., in imperial mantle.
F. Rad. and cuir. bust r.
FF. Rad. and cuir. bust l.
G. Rad., helmeted and cuir. bust l., with spear and shield.
GG. Rad., helmeted and cuir. bust l.
H. Rad. and cuir. bust r., with spear and shield.
HH. Rad. and cuir. bust l., with spear and shield.
J. Rad. and cuir. bust r., with eagle-tipped sceptre.
JJ. Rad. and cuir. bust l., with eagle-tipped sceptre.
K. Laur. and cuir. bust r., with spear and shield.
KK. Laur. and cuir. bust l., with eagle-tipped sceptre.
L. Jugate busts of emperor, in imperial mantle, r. hand raised, and Sol. holding whip, r.
LL. Jugate rad. and cuir. busts of emperor and Sol l.
M. Bare-headed full-face bust, dr. and cuir.
N. Laur. and cuir. bust r., holding globe.
NN. Laur. and cuir. bust l., holding globe.
P. Laur. and dr. bust r., holding globe.
PP. Laur. and dr. bust l., holding globe.

A

Mint-Marks.

The mint-marks of Carausius' coinage are many and various, and it has been thought best to give them here in a list similar to those of obverse legends and types above. Therefore, instead of showing each one in the usual manner, thus $\frac{S|P}{MLXXI}$, they have been tabulated below. The first column gives a serial reference number, the second the letter or letters appearing in the exergue, the third any letter appearing in the left of the field, the fourth any letter or symbol in the right of the field, and the fifth the mint to which the mark is allocated.

No.	Exergue	Left of Field	Right of Field	Mint
1				No letters in ex. or field.
2	L			London
3	ML			,,
4	ML	B	E	,,
5	ML	B	F	,,
6	ML	C	S	,,
7	ML	E	O	,,
8	ML	F	F	,,
9	ML	F	O	,,
10	ML	F	S	,,
11	ML	L		,,
12	ML	M	O	,,
13	ML		O	,,
14	ML		P	,,
15	ML	P	O	,,
16	ML	S	C	,,
17	ML	S	F	,,
18	ML	S	O	,,
19	ML	S	P	,,
20	MLX	B	B	,,
21	MLX	B	E	,,
22	MLXX	B	E	,,
23	MLXX	S	P	,,
24	MLXXI			,,
25	MLXXI	B		,,
26	MLXXI	B	B	,,
27	MLXXI	B	E	,,
28	MLXXI	B*	E	,,
29	MLXXI	B	F	,,
30	MLXXI	B	L	,,
31	MLXXI	F	B	,,
32	MLXXI	S		,,
33	MLXXI	S	C	,,
34	MLXXI	S	E	,,
35	MLXXI	S	P	,,
36	SP			,,
37	II			,,
38	III			,,
39	XI	L		,,
40	XX	F		,,
41	XX	F	O	,,
42	XXI	B	E	,,
43	BRI			Probably London
44		B		London
45		B	E	,,
46		E	O	,,

No.	Exergue	Left of Field	Right of Field	Mint
47		F	O	London
48		F	S	,,
49		L		,,
50		L	★	,,
51		L	O	,,
52			L	,,
53		O		,,
54		O	F	,,
55		S		London and Colchester
56		S	C	,, ,,
57		S	P	,, ,,
58		V		London
59		V	★	,,
60	C			Colchester
61	C	B		,,
62	C	F	O	,,
63	C	S	C	,,
64	C	S	P	,,
65	CXXI			,,
66	CXXI	B	E	,,
67		C		,,
68			C	,,
69	MC			,,
70	MC	S	P	,,
71	MCXXI			,,
72	MCXXI	B	E	,,
73	MSC			,,
74	MSCC			,,
75	MSCL			,,
76	MSXXI			,,
77	PC			,,
78	S	C	C	,,
79	S	S	C	,,
80	SC			,,
81	SC	S	C	,,
82	SMC			,,
83	SPC			,,
84	XXIC			Colchester
85	RSR			London or Richborough
86	RSS			,, ,,
87	RXR			,, ,,
88	SRS			,, ,,
89	R			Rouen
90	OPR			,,

The mint-marks of London usually contain the letter L, but some of those which do not can be attributed on style : the same remarks apply to the coins of Colchester in respect to the letter C.   The RSR-marked coins, mainly *denarii* but including some *aurei* and *antoniniani*, are usually attributed to London, but there has been a suggestion that this mark should be given to a mint at Rutupiae (Richborough) : the problem still awaits final solution.   Similarly, it has been thought by some students that the coins with C or CL as part of the mint-mark might have been issued at Clausentum (Bitterne, near Southampton), but Colchester seems, on all grounds, to be more likely.   The issues of Rouen (Rotomagus) are frequently unmarked, and sometimes have in the exergue the final letters of the reverse legend : the marks R and OPR and their barbarous variants seem definitely to be connected with a series so distinct in style that they cannot well have emanated from a British mint.

Before dealing with the coinage of Carausius, mention should be made of a medallion included by Miss Jocelyn Toynbee in her " Roman Medallions " (American Numismatic Society, Numismatic Studies, No. 5, 1944), which is probably unique, and may be a " strike " in Æ from gold-medallion dies. It is stated to have been discovered in an old collection in the North of England and is believed to have been found locally.

97a IMP C M AV CARAVSIVS P F AVG.   Laureate bust, wearing imperial mantle and holding eagle-tipped sceptre, l.

R. VICTORIA CARAVSI AVG.   Victory in biga galloping r. : in ex., I. N. P. C. D. A. Æ *medallion*, 1·4″ diameter.

No satisfactory expansion or explanation of the exergual letters has yet been suggested.

Mint of London.
N aurei.

No.	OBV. LEGEND	OBV. TYPE	REVERSE	MINT MARK	M. & S. REF.
98	41	E	CONSERVAT AVG. Jupiter stdg. l., holding thunderbolt and sceptre : before him, eagle.	3	1
99	41	E	CONSERVATORI AVGGG. Hercules standing r., wearing lion-skin, quiver on shoulder, with club and bow.	3	2
100	5	B	PAX AVG. In ex., VOT V. Pax stdg. l., with olive branch and sceptre.	1	3
101	1	B	As preceding, but with MVLT X in ex.	1	4
102	5	B or D	PAX CARAVSI AVG. Type as preceding.	1	5
103	41	E	SALVS AVGG. Salus stdg. l., feeding serpent held in her arms.	1	6

104   152   230

R denarii.

104	5	KK	ADVENTVS AVG. Emperor on horseback l., raising r. hand : to l., captive.	1, 3	7
105	7	B	CONSER AVG. Neptune seated l. on rock, holding anchor and trident.	3	8
106	27	B	VIRTVS IN or INV AVG. Emperor stdg. r., with globe and spear.	2	9

Æ antoniniani.

The coins of this denomination issued by Carausius are so numerous, and bear so many different combinations of obverse type and legend, reverse, and mint-mark, that it has been thought sufficient for the purpose of the present work to give only the reverse legends and types associated with each.

107 ADVENTVS AVG.   Type as No. 104.   *M. & S.* 10–11.
108 COHR or COHRT PRAET.   Four standards.   *M. & S.* 12.
109 COMES AVG.   Minerva stdg. l., with olive branch and spear.   *M. & S.* 13.
110 COMES AVG.   Victory stdg. l., with wreath and palm.   *M. & S.* 14–17.
111 COMES AVG.   As previous, but Victory adv. r.   *M. & S.* 18.
112 COMES AVG.   Victory stdg. r., with wreath and standard.   *M. & S.* 19.
113 COMES AVGGG.   Type as No. 109.   *M. & S.* 20.

The use of the plural AVGGG shows that Carausius employed his coinage to assert his claim to be the accepted colleague of Diocletian and Maximianus : this point will be discussed at greater length when dealing with the coins struck by Carausius in their names.

114 COMES AVGGG. Type as preceding, but Minerva holds spear and leans on shield. *M. & S.* 21.
115 CONCORD EXERCI. Four standards. *M. & S.* 22.
116 CONCO MIL or CONCORDIA MILITVM. Emperor stdg. l., holding spear and clasping hand of Concordia stdg. r. *M. & S.* 23.
117 CONCORD MI or MILIT. Clasped hands. *M. & S.* 24-25.
118 CONCORD MI. Concordia stdg. l., holding two standards. *M. & S.* 26.
119 CONCORDIA AV. Concordia stdg. l., holding sceptre. *M. & S.* 27.
120 CONCORDIA MILIT or MILITVM. Clasped hands. *M. & S.* 28.
121 CONSERVAT AVG. Sol stdg. facing, head l., raising r. hand and holding globe. *M. & S.* 29.
122 FELICIT TEMP. Felicitas standing l., holding caduceus and sceptre. *M. & S.* 30.
123 FELICITAS AVG. As preceding. *M. & S.* 31.
124 FIDEM MILIT. Fides stdg. l., holding two standards. *M. & S.* 32.
125 FIDES MILITVM. As preceding. *M. & S.* 33.
126 FORTVNA AVG. Fortuna stdg. l., with rudder and cornucopiae. *M. & S.* 34.
127 FORTVNA AVG. Fortuna stdg. l., holding anchor. *M. & S.* 35.
128 FORTVNA AVG. Fortuna seated l., holding rudder and cornucopiae. *M. & S.* 36.
129 FORTVNA AVG. Fortuna stdg. l., holding baton and cornucopiae. *M. & S.* 37.
130 GENIVS AVG. Genius standing l., holding patera and cornucopiae : to r., standard. *M. & S.* 38.
131 GERMANICVS MAX V. Trophy between two captives. *M. & S.* 39-40.
132 HILARITAS AVG. Hilaritas stdg. l., holding palm and cornucopiae. *M. & S.* 41.
133 HILARITAS AVGGG. As preceding. *M. & S.* 42-43.
134 IOVI AVGG. Jupiter standing, with thunderbolt and sceptre. *M. & S.* 44.
135 IOVI CON. Jupiter stdg. l., as preceding : at his feet, globe. *M. & S.* 45.
136 IOVI VICTORI or VICTORIA. Jupiter, l., looking r., with thunderbolt and sceptre. *M. & S.* 46.
137 LAETIT AVG. Laetitia stdg. l., with wreath and anchor, javelin or sceptre. *M. & S.* 47.
138 LAETITI AVG. As preceding. *M. & S.* 48.
139 LAETITIA AVG. As preceding. *M. & S.* 49-52.
140 LAETITIA AVG. Laetitia seated l., r. hand outstretched, l. holding sceptre. *M. & S.* 54.

The following coins, Nos. 141 to 153, are the " legionary " issues of the London mint : pieces with similar legends were also issued at Camulodunum and the mint which used the RSR signature. Like Victorinus, Carausius struck coins in honour of certain legions not actually under his control, but whose allegiance it might be politic to court in the event of any possible extension of his domains. The following table shows the legions mentioned on Carausius' coinage, with the place at which each was then stationed, and their respective badges as depicted.

Legion.	*Station.*	*Badge or Badges.*
I. Minervia	Lower Rhine	Ram
II. Augusta	Britain	Capricorn
II. Parthica	Gaul	Centaur. Boar.
IIII. Flavia	Gaul	Lion. Bust and two lions. Centaur.
VII. Claudia	Gaul	Bull
VIII. Augusta	Upper Rhine	Bull
XX. Valeria Victrix	Britain	Boar
XXII. Primigenia	Upper Rhine	Capricorn
XXX. Ulpia Victrix	Lower Rhine	Neptune

Certain legionary coins occur with blundered or incomplete legends, but these are here omitted.

141 LEG I M. Ram standing r. *M. & S.* 55.
142 LEG MI or MIN. Ram standing r. *M & S.* 56.
143 LEG II AVG. Capricorn l. *M. & S.* 57-59.
144 LEG PARTH. Female centaur walking r., holding palm. *M. & S.* 60.
145 LEG II PARTH. Male centaur walking l. *M. & S.* 61-64.
146 LEG II PARTH or PARTHICA. Boar r. or l. *M. & S.* 65.
147 LEG IIII FL. Lion r. *M. & S.* 69.
148 LEG IIII FLAVIA. Youthful diademed head, r. : below, two lions facing each other. *M. & S.* 71-72.
149 LEG VII CL or CLA. Bull r. *M. & S.* 74-76.
150 LEG VIII AVG. Bull r. *M. & S.* 77.
151 LEG XX VV. Boar r. *M. & S.* 82-83.
152 LEG IIXX PRIMIG. Capricorn l. *M. & S.* 80-81.
153 LEG XXX VLPIA or VLPIA VI. Neptune standing or seated l., holding globe, anchor or dolphin and trident. *M. & S.* 84-86.
154 MARS VICTOR. Mars adv. r., with spear and trophy. *M. & S.* 88.
155 MARS VLTOR. Mars adv. r., with spear and shield. *M. & S.* 89.
156 MARTI PACIF. Mars l., with olive-branch, spear and shield. *M. & S.* 90.
157 MONETA AVG. Moneta l., with scales and cornucopiae. *M. & S.* 91-92.
158 MONITA AVGVST. Moneta l., with scales and sceptre. *M. & S.* 93.
159 ORIEN AVG. Sol walking l., raising r. hand and holding globe. *M. & S.* 94-95.
160 ORIENS A. Sol walking l., raising r. hand and holding whip. *M. & S.* 96.
161 PACATOR ORBIS. Radiate and dr. bust of Sol r. *M. & S.* 97.
162 PAX AVG. Pax standing l., holding olive-branch and vertical sceptre. *M. & S.* 98-117.
163 PAX AVG. As preceding, but Pax holds transverse sceptre. *M. & S.* 118-124.
Nos. 162 and 163, with the corresponding issues of Camulodunum, are the commonest of all the reverse types of Carausius' *antoniniani*.
164 PAX AVG. Pax standing l., holding globe and sceptre. *M. & S.* 125-126.
165 PAX AVG. Pax standing l., holding wreath and sceptre. *M. & S.* 127.
166 PAX AVG. Pax standing l., holding two sceptres. *M. & S.* 128.
167 PAX AVG. Pax standing l., holding baton and cornucopiae. *M. & S.* 129.
168 PAX AVG. Pax standing l., holding olive-branch and cornucopiae. *M. & S.* 130.
169 PAX AVG. Pax standing l., holding caduceus and cornucopiae. *M. & S.* 131.
170 PAX AVG. Pax seated l., holding patera and cornucopiae. *M. & S.* 132.
171 PAX AVG. Minerva stdg. l., holding spear and Victory on globe. *M. & S.* 133.
172 PAX AVG. Soldier standing r., with spear and shield. *M. & S.* 134.
173 PAX AVG. Victory l., with wreath and palm. *M. & S.* 137.
174 PAX AVGG. Type as No. 162. *M. & S.* 138-139.
175 PAX AVGG. Type as No. 163. *M. & S.* 140.
176 PAX AVGGG. Type as No. 162. *M. & S.* 141-142.
177 PAX AVGGG. Type as No. 163. *M. & S.* 143-144.
178 PAX AVGGG. Pax standing l., holding Victory on globe, and sceptre. *M. & S.* 145.
179 PAX CARAVSI AVG. Type as No. 163. *M. & S.* 146.
180 PIAETAS AVG. Pietas standing l., sacrificing at altar. *M. & S.* 147.
181 PROVID AVGGG. Providentia stdg. l., holding baton and cornucopiae, globe at her feet. *M. & S.* 148.
182 PROVIDENT AVG. Providentia stdg. l., holding globe and sceptre. *M. & S.* 149-150.
183 PROVIDENTIA AVGG. Type as No. 181. *M. & S.* 151.
184 PROVIDENTIA AVGGG. Type as No. 181. *M. & S.* 152.
185 SAECVLI FELICIT. Emperor standing r., holding spear and globe. *M. & S.* 153.
186 SALVS AVG. Salus stdg. l., feeding serpent rising from altar, and holding sceptre. *M. & S.* 154-157.
187 SALVS AVG. As preceding, but Salus holds cornucopiae. *M. & S.* 159.
188 SALVS AVG. Pax l., with olive-branch and sceptre. *M. & S.* 160.
189 SALVS AVG. Salus r., feeding serpent held in her arms. *M. & S.* 161.
190 SALVS AVG. Salus l., beside altar, with patera and sceptre. *M. & S.* 162.
191 SALVS AVG. Aesculapius l., holding serpent-staff. *M. & S.* 163.
192 SALVS AVGGG. Type as No. 189. *M. & S.* 164.
193 SALVS PVBLICA. As preceding. *M. & S.* 165-6.
194 SECVRIT PERP. Securitas l., leaning on column, r. hand raised, legs crossed. *M. & S.* 167-9.
195 SOLI INVICT. Sol in quadriga galloping l. *M. & S.* 170.
196 TEMP FELIC. Felicitas l., with caduceus and cornucopiae. *M. & S.* 171.

197 TEMPORVM FELICITAS. As preceding. *M. & S.* 172.
198 VICTORIA AVG. Victory l., with sceptre and palm ; at her feet, altar. *M. & S.* 173.
199 VICTORIA AVG. Victory adv. l., with wreath and palm ; sometime with captive at her feet. *M. & S.* 174.
200 VICTORIA AVG. As preceding, but Victory r. *M. & S.* 175-6.
201 VICTORIA AVG. Victory l. on globe between two captives, with wreath and palm. *M. & S.* 177.
202 VICTORIA GERM. Trophy between two captives. *M. & S.* 178.
203 VIRTVS AVG. Mars standing r. with spear and shield. *M. & S.* 179.
204 VIRTVS AVG. Mars adv. r., with spear and shield. *M. & S.* 180.
205 VIRTVS AVG. Mars adv. r., with spear and trophy. *M. & S.* 181.
206 VIRTVS AVGGG. Type as No. 203. *M. & S.* 182-4.

Mint of Colchester (Camulodunum).

Æ denarii.

No.	Obv. Legend	Obv. Type	Reverse	Mint Mark	M. & S. Ref.
207	5	B or D	CONCORDIA MILITVM. Clasped hands.	60	186
208	5	D	LEG IIII FL . . . . Centaur walking l., holding club transversely with both hands.	60	187

Æ antoniniani.

Many of the types struck by the London mint are also found with the signature of Camulodunum : they are therefore not listed here, but their appropriate reference numbers are quoted, as follows :—Nos. 107, 110-113, 116, 117, 125, 126, 128, 132, 137-139, 145, 149, 154, 157, 159-160, 162, 163, 168, 174, 176, 177, 181, 186, 189, 197, 199, 203, 205 and 206.

209 ABVNDANTIA AVG. Abundantia stdg. l., emptying cornucopiae into modius. *M. & S.* 189.
210 APOLINI CON AV. Griffin walking l. *M. & S.* 192.
211 APOLLI or APOLLINI CO, CON or CONS, sometimes with A, AV or AVG. Type as preceding. *M. & S.* 193-6.
212 APOLLINI . . . Apollo seated l., holding olive-branch. *M. & S.* 197.
213 CONCORDIA AVGGG. Two emperors, togate, standing face to face, clasping hands. *M. & S.* 204.
214 CONSERVAT AV. Hercules stdg. l., with lion-skin and club. *M. & S.* 212.
215 CONSERVAT AVG. Neptune seated l., holding anchor and trident. *M. & S.* 213-4.
216 CONSERVATOR. Jupiter stdg. l., holding globe and sceptre. *M. & S.* 214a.
217 CONSTANT AVG. Nude male figure stdg. r., head l., with sceptre. *M. & S.* 215.
218 EXPECTATE VENI. Britannia standing r., holding ensign or trident, clasping hand of emperor standing l., holding sceptre. *M. & S.* 216-8.
219 EXPECTATE VEENI. Type as preceding. *M. & S.* 219.
220 FELICIT PVBL or PVBLI. Felicitas l., leaning on column and holding caduceus. *M. & S.* 220.
221 FELICITAS AVG. Galley with mast and rowers on waves. *M. & S.* 221.
222 FELICITAS SAECVL. Emperor r., with spear and globe. *M. & S.* 222.
223 FIDES EXERCIT. Four standards. *M. & S.* 223.
224 FIDES MILIT or MILITV. Type as preceding. *M. & S.* 229.
225 FIDES MILIT. Fides seated l., holding globe in patera and cornucopiae. *M. & S.* 230.
226 FIDES MILITVM. Clasped hands. *M. & S.* 231.
227 FORTVNA. Fortuna seated l. on wheel, holding rudder and cornucopiae. *M. & S.* 232-4.
228 FORTVNA RED, REDV or RAEDVX. Type as preceding. *M. & S.* 237-9.
229 GENIO BRITANNI. Youthful Genius stdg. l. before altar, holding patera and cornucopiae. *M. & S.* 240.
230 GENIVS EXERCIT. Type as preceding, but without altar. *M. & S.* 241-2.
231 IOVI CONSE or CONSER. Jupiter stdg. l., holding thunderbolt and sceptre or caduceus. *M. & S.* 244.
232 IOVI CONSERV AV. Type as preceding. *M. & S.* 245.
233 LAETITIA AVG. Galley r., with rowers ; sometimes with mast and cordage ; sometimes on waves. *M. & S.* 264-5.
234 LAETITIA AVGGG. Laetitia stdg. l. holding wreath and anchor or javelin. *M. & S.* 266-7.

235 LEG I MIN. Ram standing r. *M. & S.* 268.
236 LEG IIII FLA or FLAVIA. Centaur walking r. or l., holding sceptre, javelin or standard. *M. & S.* 272-3.
237 LEG XX AVG. Boar l. *M. & S.* 275.
238 LIBERALITAS AVG. Emperor seated l. on platform, holding branch : behind him, prefect l. : to r., Liberalitas l. with tessera and cornucopiae : to l., citizen ascending steps. *M. & S.* 277-8.
239 MARTI PACIFE or PACIFERO. Mars l., with olive-branch, spear and shield. *M. & S.* 281-3.

240 248 250

240 MONETA AVGGG. Type as No. 157. *M. & S.* 291.
241 MONITA AVG. Type as No. 157. *M. & S.* 292.
242 PAX AVG. Pax adv. r., with olive-branch and sceptre. *M. & S.* 325.
243 PAX AVG. Pax adv. l., with olive-branch and sometimes sceptre. *M. & S.* 326-8.
244 PAX AVG. Pax standing l., holding wreath and baton, javelin or rudder. *M. & S.* 329.
245 PAX AVG. Pax l., with globe and cornucopiae. *M. & S.* 332.
246 PAX AVGVSTI. Type as No. 243. *M. & S.* 341.
247 PIETAS AVG. Pietas l., sacrificing at altar. *M. & S.* 342.
248 PIETAS AVGGG. Mercury l., with purse and caduceus. *M. & S.* 343.
249 PROVI AVG. Providentia l., with baton and cornucopiae. *M. & S.* 344.
250 PROVID AVG. As preceding, but globe at feet. *M. & S.* 345-352.
251 PROVID AVG. As preceding, but holding globe and cornucopiae. *M. & S.* 353-6.
252 PROVID AVG. As preceding, but with globe and sceptre. *M. & S.* 357-9.
253 PROVID AVG. As preceding, but with corn-ears and cornucopiae. *M. & S.* 360.
254 PROVID AVGG. Type as No. 250. *M. & S.* 361.
255 PROVID AVGGG. Type as No. 251. *M. & S.* 367-370.
256 PROVID AVGGG. Type as No. 252. *M. & S.* 371-2.
257 PROVIDE AVG. Type as No. 250. *M. & S.* 373.
258 PROVIDE AVG. Type as No. 251. *M. & S.* 374-5.
259 PROVIDEN AVG. Type as No. 250. *M. & S.* 376-7.
260 PROVIDEN AVGGG. Type as No. 251. *M. & S.* 378.
261 PROVID DE. Providentia r., holding two standards, before emperor l., raising r. hand and holding globe. *M. & S.* 379.
262 PROVID DEOR. Type as previous, but second figure radiate. *M. & S.* 380.
263 PROVIDENTIA AVG. Type as No. 250. *M. & S.* 381.
264 RENOVAT ROM or ROMA. She-wolf r., suckling Romulus and Remus. *M. & S.* 382.
265 RESTIT SAECVL. Emperor l., with globe and spear, being crowned by Victory l. holding palm. *M. & S.* 385-6.
266 ROMAE AETER or AETERN. Roma seated l., holding Victory and sceptre. *M. & S.* 387-8.
267 ROMAE AETER. Roma seated in temple. *M. & S.* 389.
268 ROMAE AETERNAE. Roma seated l. on shield, presenting Victory to Emperor standing r. with spear. *M. & S.* 390.
269 SAECVLARES AVG. Lion r. *M. & S.* 391-2.
270 SAECVLARES AVG. Cippus inscr. COS IIII. *M. & S.* 393.
271 SAECVLI FELICITA. Emperor r., with spear and globe. *M. & S.* 395.
272 SALVS AVG. Salus seated l., holding sceptre and feeding serpent rising from altar. *M. & S.* 401.
273 SALVS AVG. As preceding, without sceptre. *M. & S.* 403.
274 SALVS AVGGG. As preceding. *M. & S.* 404-5.
275 SECVRITAS AV. Securitas l., leaning on column, legs crossed. *M. & S.* 406.
276 SOLI INVI. Sol r., between two seated captives, raising r. hand and holding globe. *M. & S.* 407.
277 SOLI INVICTO. Sol in quadriga galloping l. *M. & S.* 408-9.
278 SPES AVG. Victory l., with wreath and palm. *M. & S.* 410.

279 SPES PVBL, PVBLIC or PVBLICA.   Spes walking l., holding flower. *M. & S.* 411-7.
280 TEMP FELICIT.   Felicitas l., with sceptre and cornucopiae. *M. & S.* 418.
281 TEMPORVM FEL, FELI, FELIC, FELICIT or FELICITAS.   As preceding, but with caduceus instead of sceptre, and sometimes without cornucopiae. *M. & S.* 419-423.
282 VICTOR AVG.   Victory r., with wreath and palm. *M. & S.* 424.
283 VICTORIA AV or AVG.   Victory l., with wreath and palm, sometimes with captive at foot and sometimes with standard instead of palm. *M. & S.* 426-430.
284 VICTORIA AVG.   Mars walking r., with spear. *M. & S.* 431.
285 VICTORIA GERMA.   Trophy between two captives. *M. & S.* 432.
286 VIRTVS AVG.   Lion r. *M. & S.* 435.
287 VIRTVS AVGG.   Mars l., r. hand on shield, l. holding spear. *M. & S.* 442.
288 VIRTVS AVGGG.   Mars as preceding, r. or l. *M. & S.* 443.
289 VIRTVTI AVG.   Hercules r., strangling lion. *M. & S.* 444.

The following coin, found at Magna Castra Farm, Kenchester, is published in *Num. Chron.*, Vol. XIX, 5th Series, 1939, p. 291. The legends are incomplete, but the reverse seems to be otherwise unrecorded, and the mint-mark C is certain.

289a IMP CARAVSIVS [? P F AVG]. *Obv.* type C.

R.   VOT SVSC — — — AVG IIII (?).   Togate figure standing l., holding patera over altar : in ex., C.

Dr. C. H. V. Sutherland, in his note on the coin, mentions that as the letters following *Vot Susc.* are lost, the termination *Aug. IIII* is difficult of explanation, unless the missing portion of the legend contained a numeral such as XX and the remainder of the legend is an attempt to represent AVG IMP.

Coins with mint-mark S, SC or SP in field.

Æ antoniniani.

The following reverses are found with mint-marks Nos. 55, 56 or 57 ; but the reverse types Nos. 125, 136, 137-9, 154, 157, 159, 162-4, 169, 175, 176, 182, 190, 192, 203-5, 234, 239, 251, 254, 255, 257, 258, 271, 279 and 281 are also recorded with these three mint marks.   The place of issue is not certain, but most of the pieces so marked may be adjudged to London on style.

290 ABVNDENTIA AVG.   Abundantia stdg. l., dropping fruits from hand. *M. & S.* 445.
291 COMES AVG.   Neptune l. on prow and dolphin, with dolphin and trident. *M. & S.* 446.
292 COMIS AVG.   Victory l., with wreath and palm. *M. & S.* 447.
293 CONSERVAT AVG.   Jupiter r., holding spear. *M. & S.* 448.
294 FORTVNA REDVX.   Fortuna l., with rudder on globe and cornucopiae. *M. & S.* 450.
295 FORTVNAE.   Fortuna seated l., with rudder and cornucopiae. *M. & S.* 451.
296 IOVI CONSERV, CONSERVA or CONSERVAT.   Jupiter l., with thunderbolt and sceptre. *M. & S.* 453.
297 MARTI AVG.   Mars l., with spear. *M. & S.* 464.
298 MERC CON AVG.   Mercury l., with ʼpurse and caduceus. *M. & S.* 468.
299 MONET AVG.   Moneta l., with scales and cornucopiae. *M. & S.* 469.
300 NEPTVNO REDVCI.   Neptune l., with dolphin and trident. *M. & S.* 472.
301 PAX AVG.   Pax l., holding patera over altar, cornucopiae and rudder. *M. & S.* 492.
302 PAX AVG.   Providentia l., holding baton and cornucopiae : at feet, globe. *M. & S.* 493.

Coins with SP in exergue.

Æ antoniniani.

The following, Nos. 303 and 304, bear mint-mark No. 36, and are attributed to London.

303 VICTORIV CARAVSI AV.   Three winged Victories standing l., the first and second holding wreaths, the third wreath and palm. *M. & S.* 530.
304 VICTOR or VICTORIA GERMAN.   Trophy between two captives. *M. & S.* 531-2.

Coins with RSR mint-mark.

N aurei.

Variants of mint-mark indicated where necessary.

No.	OBV. LEGEND	OBV. TYPE	REVERSE	MINT MARK	M. & S. REF.
305	1	B	LEG IIII FEL. Lion walking r., with thunderbolt in mouth.	85	533
306	49	G	ROMANO RENOVA. She-wolf l., suckling Romulus and Remus.	85	534

R denarii.

No.	OBV. LEGEND	OBV. TYPE	REVERSE	MINT MARK	M. & S. REF.
307	5	BB, D or F	ADVENTVS AVG. Emperor riding l., r. hand raised, holding sceptre ; sometimes captive to l.	85	535
308	6	D	As preceding.	85	536
309	34	B	As preceding.	85	538
310	5	D	ADVENTVS AVG. Emperor riding r., spear over head, enemy under horse.	85	540
311	5	B or D	ADVENTVS AVGG. Type as preceding.	85	541
312	36	BB	CLARIT CARAVSI AVG. Rad. and dr. bust of Sol r. (attributed to this mint by Sir John Evans).	1	542
313	9	E	CONCOR MI. Clasped hands.	85	543
314	5	BB	CONCORD MILIT. Concordia l., holding two standards.	85	544
315	5	B	CONCORDIA AVGG. Type as No. 313.	85	545
316	7	B	CONCORDIA AVGG. Type as No. 313.	85	546
317	1	B	CONCORDIA MTLITVM. Type as No. 313.	85	547
318	5	B, BB or D	CONCORDIA MILIT or MILITVM. Type as No. 313.	85	548
319	6	B or D	As preceding.	85	549
320	9	B	As preceding.	85	550
321	5	D	CONCORDIA [MILIT]. Emperor standing r., clasping hand of Concordia standing l.	85	551
322	5	B	CONSER AV. Neptune seated l. on rock, holding anchor and trident.	85	552
323	6	B	As preceding.	85	553

No.	OBV. LEGEND	OBV. TYPE	REVERSE	MINT MARK	M. & S. REF.
324	5	B	EXPECTAT or EXPECTATE VFNI. Britannia standing r., holding standard or trident, clasping hand of emperor stdg. l., holding sceptre.	85	554
325	6	B or D	As preceding.	85	555
326	5	B	EXPECTATI. Type as preceding.	85	556
327	6	B	As preceding.	85	557
328	37	P	EXPECTATI VENIES. Type as preceding.	85	558
329	5	·B	FEDES MILITVM. Fides stdg. l., holding two standards.	85	559
330	5	B, BB or D	FELICITA AV or AVG, FELICITAS or FELICITAS AVG. Galley.	85	560
331	36	B	As preceding.	85	561
332	36	B	FIDE MI AV. Fides stdg. r., holding standard, and clasping hand of emperor standing l.	85	562
333	5	B	FIDEM MILITV. Moneta l., with scales and cornucopiae.	1	563
334	5	B or D	FIDES MILIT. Type as No. 329.	85	564
335	6	D	[F] ORTVNA AVG. Bust of Fortuna r. in wreath, holding olive-branch (?): behind her, a flower.	1	565

This is the celebrated coin which Stukeley read as ORIVNA AVG, and from which he deduced the existence of the Empress Oriuna, wife of Carausius. All known specimens are faulty as regards the first letter of the legend, but FORTVNA AVG is certain, and Oriuna remains a figment of Stukeley's fertile imagination.

No.	OBV. LEGEND	OBV. TYPE	REVERSE	MINT MARK	M. & S. REF.
336	19	B	FORTVNA AVG. Fortuna seated l. on wheel, with rudder and cornucopiae.	85	567
337	5	B	LEG IIII FL. Lion walking l., thunderbolt in mouth.	85	568
338	1	BB	ORIENS AVG. Sun-god l., raising r. hand and holding globe.	85	569
339	5	B or D	As preceding.	85	570
340	5	B or D	RENOVAT ROMA, ROMAN, ROMANO or RVMANO. Wolf and twins.	85	571
341	5, 6 or 8	B, D or E	ROMANO RENA, RENO, RENOV or RENOVA. Type as preceding.	85, 86 or 87	572-4
342	49	G, with helmet laureate	As preceding.	85	577
343	5	D	ROMANOR RENOV. As preceding.	85	577a
344	5	D	ROMAE AETER or AETERNAE. Roma seated in temple.	85	578
345	5	B	ROME HERC. Victory crowning Hercules in temple.	85	579
346	9	B	TEMPORVM FEL. Felicitas l., with caduceus and cornucopiae.	85	580
347	5	D	VBERITA AV or AVG. Woman milking cow r.	85	581
348	9	PP	As preceding.	85	582
349	36	BB	As preceding.	85	583
350	5 or 9	D or B	VBERTA, VBERTAS or VBERSTA AV or AVG. Type as preceding, sometimes to l.	85	584-5
351	37	BB	As preceding.	SR	586
352	36	BB	VBERITAS AVG. Uberitas stdg. r., holding standard, clasping hand of soldier l., holding spear.	85	589
353	37	PP	As preceding.	85	590
354	5 or 6	B or D	VIRTVS AVG. Lion walking l., thunderbolt in mouth.	85	591-2
355	5	D	VIRTVS AVG. Emperor l., raising r. hand and holding spear.	1	593
356	5	B or D	VOTO, or VOTVM, PVBLIC, PVBLICO or PVBLICVM. Altar inscr. MVLTIS XX IMP in three or four lines.	85	595 and 597
357	5	D	VOTO PVBLICO MVLTIS XX IMP in four lines in wreath.	85	596

Æ antoniniani.

The coins of this denomination with RSR mint-mark include reverse types already listed and numbered 104, 117, 120, 157, 210, 218, 266, 281, 340, 341, 350, 352 and 357, and also the following :—

358 CONCORDIA AVG. Clasped hands. *M. & S.* 602.
359 FELICITAS. Galley r., with mast and rowers. *M. & S.* 607.
360 FIDES MILITVM. Fides l., holding ensign. *M. & S.* 608.

Mint of Rotomagus (Rouen).

As has been previously noted, the issues of this mint are so distinct in style from those of London and Colchester that there should be no mistaking them. The portraits of the emperor are narrow and conventional, and clearly to be distinguished from the burly thick-necked Carausius depicted by the British mints : the lettering is poor and the legends often blundered.

The attribution of the series to Rouen is certain : not only did a large hoard found in Rouen consist entirely of these coins, but they occur in other parts of Northern France. They are scarce in British hoards, although sometimes found.

No.	Obv. Legend	Obv. Type	Reverse	Mint Mark	M. &. S. Ref.
N aurei.					
361	9	B	CONCORDIA MILITV. Concordia l., holding two ensigns.	VL	621
362	1	E	CONCORDIA MILITVM. Emperor standing r. joining hands with Concordia standing l.	VM	622
363	1	EE	As preceding.	VM	623
364	9	B	As preceding.	VM	624

Æ antoniniani.

365 AEQVITAS MVNDI. Aequitas l., with scales and cornucopiae. *M. & S.* 627.
366 ECVITAS MVNDI. Type as No. 362. *M. & S.* 629-632.
367 CONCOR MILIT. Type as No. 362. *M. & S.* 634.
368 FELICITAS A or AVG. Type as preceding : in ex., OPR. *M. & S.* 636.
369 FIDES MILITVM. Emperor r., clasping hand of Fides l. *M. & S.* 637.
370 FORTVNA AVG. Fortuna l., with baton or rudder and cornucopiae. *M. & S.* 638-640.
371 FORTVNA RE, RED or REDV. Fortuna l., holding rudder or wheel and cornucopiae. *M. & S.* 641-3.
372 FORTVNA RED or REDV. Fortuna l., sacrificing at altar. *M. & S.* 644.
373 FORTVNA REDV. Fortuna seated l. on wheel, holding rudder and cornucopiae. *M. & S.* 645-6.
374 FORTVNAE. Fortuna l., holding wheel and cornucopiae. *M. & S.* 647.
375 LAETITIA. Galley r. : sometimes in ex., OPA. *M. & S.* 648-649a.
376 PAX EXERCITI. Pax l., with olive-branch and standard : in ex., XXI. *M. & S.* 650.
377 PROVID . . ., PROVIDE AVG, PROVIDEN or PROVIDEN AVG. Providentia l., with globe and sceptre : sometimes in field, x. *M. & S.* 652-4.
378 PROVIDENT, PROVIDEN AVG, or PROVIDENTIA. Sometimes with AV. Providentia l., holding corn-ears and sceptre : sometimes in ex., IIE or IIG. *M. & S.* 655-7.
379 PROVIDENTIA AV. Providentia facing, holding baton and cornucopiae. *M. & S.* 658.
380 PROVIDENTIA (or PROVIDENTIA) AVG. Providentia l., holding globe, branch, or corn-ears and sceptre. *M. & S.* 659.
381 ROMAE AETER. Roma seated l. on shield, holding globe and sceptre. *M. & S.* 660-1.
382 SALVS AVG. Salus l., feeding serpent rising from altar, and holding cornucopiae : sometimes in ex., R. *M. & S.* 662-4.
383 SALVS AVG. Salus l., sacrificing at altar with patera, and holding cornucopiae : sometimes in ex., R. *M. & S.* 665-6.
384 SALVS AVG. Salus l., feeding serpent coiled round staff, and holding sceptre or cornucopiae. *M. & S.* 667-670.
385 SALVS AVGG. Salus l., sacrificing at altar. *M. & S.* 671.
386 SALVS III, or IIII AVG. Type as No. 382. *M. & S.* 672-3.
387 SECVRITAS PER or PERP. Securitas l., leaning on column, legs crossed : sometimes in ex., OP. *M. & S.* 674-677.
388 TEMPORVM F, FEL, FELI, or FELILIT. Felicitas l., with caduceus and cornucopiae. *M. & S.* 678-681.
389 TVTELA or TVTELA AVG. Tutela l. beside altar, holding patera, wreath or flower and cornucopiae, or sceptre : sometimes in ex., IOI. *M. & S.* 682-689.
390 TVTELA AVG. As preceding, but holding anchor with broken shaft. *M. & S.* 690.
391 TVTELA DIVI AVG. Tutela l., with patera and cornucopiae. *M. & S.* 691.
392 TVTELA P. Tutela l., holding flower and cornucopiae. *M. & S.* 692-4.

393

393 VIRT or VIRTV AVG. Hercules wearing lion-skin standing r., clasping hand of female figure standing l. and holding cornucopiae : between them, altar : sometimes in ex., Λ or XX. *M. & S.* 695.

394 VIRTVS AVG. Mars standing l., holding Victory on globe and spear or leaning on shield. *M. & S.* 696-8.

395 VIRTVS AVG. Minerva standing l., leaning on shield and holding spear. *M. & S.* 699.

396 VIRTVS IV AVG. Mars l., holding spear and leaning on shield. *M. & S.* 700.

In addition to the coins of Carausius listed above, the attribution of which is certain, or reasonably so, there are many coins which bear no mint-marks whatever. Many of these must be early issues and attributable to London, a few seem to be of Colchester, and some obviously barbarous. Most of the coins in the class are antoniniani, but there are a few denarii, which are probably of London. The types are normally identical with, or variants of, those given above, but others appear to be mere copies of the coins of earlier emperors. A complete list of them would be long, but the following are quoted here as being of interest :—

397 Æ *denarius*. ℞ PRINCIPI IVVENT. Youth in military dress standing l., holding olive-branch and sceptre. *M. & S.* 721.

Æ antoniniani.

398 HERC DEVSENIENSI (retrograde). Hercules standing r., leaning on club and pouring libation. *M. & S.* 800.

399 IOVI STATORI. Jupiter standing l., with thunderbolt and sceptre. *M. & S.* 814.

400 TEMPORVM FELICITAS. The four Seasons, as children playing. *M. & S.* 1016.

This division of the coinage of Carausius may fittingly be closed by the following coin, which was found at Magna Castra Farm, Kenchester, and is now in the Ashmolean Museum : a complete account of the piece will be found in *Num. Chron.*, Fifth Series, Vol. XVII, 1937, pp. 306-9.

400a VIRTVS CARAVSI. Helmeted and cuirassed bust l.

℞. PACATRI X AVG. Galley to l., with rowers and superstructure at stern : upon the latter, an eagle l., with wings open and wreath in beak : in ex., CANC.

Æ *antoninianus.*

Dr. C. H. V. Sutherland, in discussing this coin and the problems it raises, suggests that the ship depicted may be the flagship of Carausius' fleet, and that the legend and type refer to the victory of Carausius over Maximianus in 289 ; but the meaning of the exergual inscription is obscure and no satisfactory explanation of it has yet been offered.

———❖———

Note. Reference to the two unique medallions of Carausius will be found in the Introduction on pp. iv—vi

Chapter VI : The Coinage of Carausius—(*continued*).

Carausius, firmly seated on the throne of Britain, was not, however, suffered to rule unchallenged. During the winter of 288-9, Maximianus caused a great fleet to be prepared in the rivers of the Low Countries, and early in 289 an attempt was made to invade the island. But Carausius had expected some such attack and made preparations to meet it, and the forces of the central government could avail nothing in the face of the seamanship of the British ruler and the warlike skill of his men. History does not relate how and where the fleet of Maximianus was defeated, but defeated it certainly was, and Maximianus was compelled to make peace with Carausius, the latter being permitted to style himself co-emperor. It seems probable that after the Peace of 289 Carausius established his mint at Rouen.

The Peace of 289 supplies us with the only certain numismatic milestone of the reign, for after it began the issues of coins with the reverse legends PAX AVGGG, VIRTVS AVGGG and so on, the triple termination implying the three Augusti, Diocletian, Maximianus and Carausius. It is possible, of course, to make some tentative division of the earlier coinage into periods : many of the first issues would probably be without any mint-signature, and the mark ML has been attributed to the year 288, to be followed by coins carrying also letters in the reverse field as well as, or instead of, in the exergue. The coins struck after the Peace of 289 are usually larger than the earlier ones, and the mark of value, XXI, begins to be used.

Carausius' chief innovation was the issue of silver denarii, which, though poor in style and quality at first, seem to show a gradual improvement both in make and silver content until the later specimens are not only well struck but are composed of very good silver. It is probable that these denarii were not issued after 290. The resumption of trade and other communications with Gaul, where little or no silver was circulating, would soon have drained the island of its supplies of silver had the coinage in that metal been continued ; and Carausius, or his ministers, took care that this adverse exchange should not occur.

There is no record of the terms of the treaty concluded by Carausius with Diocletian and Maximianus, nor indeed is it certain that a formal treaty was ever drawn up, but Carausius took advantage of the agreement to issue not only the coins with AVGGG on their reverse legends mentioned above, but a series of pieces proclaiming even more clearly his acceptance as their official colleague. Chief of these coins is the following *antoninianus* of Camulodunum :—

401 CARAVSIVS ET FRATRES SVI. Jugate, radiate and cuirassed busts of Carausius, Diocletian and Maximianus, l. Maximianus is always radiate, but the others are sometimes laureate. On some specimens all three are shown with right hands raised.

℞. PAX AVGGG. Type as No. 162 or 163, mint-mark No. 64. *M. & S.* 1.

The following antoninianus must also belong to the same period :—

402 C VAL DIO . . . . AVGGG. Type similar to preceding, but the order of emperors reversed : all are radiate and have right hands raised.

℞. PAX AVGGG. Type as No. 162, mint-mark as preceding. *M. & S.* 2.

From the Drabble sale, 1939 : now in the collection of R. Cyril Lockett, Esq.

In addition to the coins depicting Carausius with his " brothers," an extensive series was struck by the British emperor for each of his colleagues, with appropriate portrait, which will now be described.

Coins issued in the name of Diocletian.

Obverse legends :—

1. IMP C DIOCLETIANVS P F AVG
2. IMP C DIOCLETIANVS P AVG
3. IMP C DIOCLETIANVS NG
4. IMP C DIOCLETIANVS AVG
5. IMP DIOCLETIANVS P F AVG
6. IMP C VAL DIOCLETIANVS AVG
7. IMP DIOCLETIANVS P AVG
8. IMP C C VAL DIOCLETIANVS P F AVG
9. IMP DIOCLETIANVS AVG
10. DIOCLETIANVS P F AVG

Obverse types and mint-marks are as for Carausius, in the foregoing tables.

Mint of London.

Æ antoniniani.

No.	Obv. Legend	Obv. Type	Reverse	Mint Mark	M. & S. Ref.
403	1	A. C. or F.	CONSERVAT AVGGG. Hercules r., resting r. hand on club and holding apples or globe.	35	3
404	4	F	LAETITIA AVGGG. Laetitia l. holding wreath and baton or anchor.	35	4
405	1	A or F	PAX AVGGG. Type as No. 162.	19 or 24	5
406	4	F	As preceding.	35	6
407	3	F _	As preceding.	35	7
408	10	A	As preceding.	35	8
409	1	A or F	PAX AVGGG. Type as No. 163.	35	9
410	4	F	As preceding.	35	10
411	5	F	As preceding.	24	11
412	1	F	PROVIDENTIA AVGGG. Providentia standing l., holding baton and cornucopiae : at feet, globe.	35	12
413	6	F	SALVS AVGGG. Salus standing l., feeding serpent rising from altar, and holding sceptre.	35	13
414	8	A	SALVS AVGGG. Salus standing r., feeding serpent held in her arms.	24	14
415	1	F	VIRTVS AVGGG. Mars standing r. with spear, leaning on shield.	35	15
416	1	F	VIRTVS AVGGG. Trophy between two seated captives.	35	16

Mint of Camulodunum.

Æ antoniniani.

417	4	F	FIDES MILITVM. Four standards.	83	17
418	1	A	As No. 404.	64	18
419	2	F	As No. 405.	64	19
420	4	F	As preceding.	64	20
421	8	F	As preceding.	64	21
422	2	F	PROVID AVGGG. Providentia standing l., as on No. 412.	64	22
423	4	F	As preceding.	64	23
424	7	F	As preceding.	64	24
425	4	C	PROVID AVGG. Providentia l., holding globe and sceptre.	64	25
426	1	F	SALVS AVG. Salus standing l., feeding serpent held in her arms.	57 (?)	26
427	2	F	SPES PVBL. Spes walking l., holding flower.	64	27
428	9	F	VICTORIA AVGGG. Victory walking l., with wreath and palm.	64	28

No.	OBV. LEGEND	OBV. TYPE	REVERSE	MINT MARK	M. & S. REF.
429	2	C	VIRTVS AVGGG. Mars standing l., holding spear and leaning on shield.	64	29
430	7	A	As preceding, but Mars r.	64	30

The mint-mark of the following coin has not been published, but the type is attributed to Camulodunum on style.

| 431 | 8 | C | VICTORIA AVGGG. Two emperors clasping hands ; between them, Victory with her hands on their shoulders. | | 31 |

Coins issued in the name of Maximianus I. Herculeus.

Obverse legends :—

1. IMP C MAXIMIANVS P F AVG
2. IMP C MAXIMIANVS P AVG
3. IMP C M A VAL MAXIMAINVS P F AVG
4. IMP C MAXIMIANVS AVG
5. IMP MAXIMIANVS P F AVG
6. MAXIMIANVS P F AVG
7. IMP C M A VAL MAXIMIANVS AVG
8. IMP C M VAL MAXIMIANVS AVG

Obverse types and mint-marks are as for Carausius, in the foregoing tables, but with bust of Maximian.

Mint of London.

N aureus.

| 432 | 6 | E | SALVS AVGGG. Salus standing r., feed-serpent held in her arms. | 3 | 32 |

Æ antoniniani.

433	1	F	COMES AVGGG. Minerva l., holding branch and spear. *Ashmolean Museum, Evans collection.*	24	—
433a	1	C	HILARITAS AVGGG. Hilaritas standing l., holding palm and cornucopiae.	35	33
434	1	C or F	PAX AVGGG. Type as No. 162 or No. 163.	35	34
435	4	F	As preceding.	35	35
436	5	F	As preceding.	35	36
437	1	F	PROVIDENTIA AVGGG. Providentia standing l., holding baton and cornucopiae.	35	37
438	1	F	SALVS AVGGG. Type as No. 432.	35	38
439	1	F	VIRTVS AVGGG. Type as No. 429 or No. 430.	35	39

Mint of Camulodunum.

Æ antoniniani.

440	1	F	MONETA AVGGG. Moneta standing l., holding scales and cornucopiae.	64	40
441	3	F	PAX AVG. Type as No. 162.	64	41
442	1	C or F	PAX AVGGG. As preceding.	64	42
443	2	F	PAX AVGGG. Type as No. 163.	64	43
444	4	F	PAX AVGGG. Type as No. 162.	64	44
445	7	F	As preceding.	64	45
446	8	F	As preceding.	64	46
447	1	GG but to r.	P AX AVGGG. Type as No. 163.	64	47
448	1	GG	As preceding.	64	48
449	1	F	PROVID AVGGG. Providentia standing l., holding baton and cornucopiae : at feet, globe.	64	49

The Peace of 289, in commemoration of which Carausius issued these coins, was not for long respected by the Romans, and, indeed, it is probable that they never intended to do so any longer than was necessary.   It is known that the town of Boulogne, which was being held by Carausius in 292, was besieged by Constantius Chlorus the following year.   Constantius was the newly-appointed " Caesar " or heir-designate of Maximianus, and he seems to have considered it his first task to restore Britain to the central government.   The town proved to be impregnable as long as its sea communications with Britain remained open, but Constantius had a palisade—perhaps some kind of boom—drawn across the entrance of the harbour, and the garrison of Boulogne was compelled to surrender the town, thus depriving Carausius of his footing in Gaul.   This, for the moment, was the total of Constantius' success, for Carausius was still able to maintain his hold on his island empire ; but sometime in the year 293 the gallant emperor, who had, in the words of the historian, " during seven years with the greatest bravery maintained and kept for himself Britain," was treacherously murdered by, or with the connivance of, his minister Allectus.

————:————

Chapter VII : The Reign of Allectus, 293-296 A.D.

Of Allectus we know little more than can be learned from his coins, for his origin and early life are unrecorded. The name " Allectus " does not occur elsewhere in Roman history or epigraphy, and it has been suggested that it is a Latin version of some Keltic word related to Alyth and perhaps the origin of McAlloit. This theory is quite incapable of verification, and to the present writer it would appear that " Allectus " may equally well be a form of " Alexius," and the man a Levantine Greek by descent. More probable is Dr. Ian A. Richmond's suggestion that the name may be derived from " Adlectus," " the chosen one."

History does not tell us of the exact position held by Allectus under Carausius, he being variously described as companion, henchman, or first minister, but it is probable that he was concerned with administration and finance, military affairs being kept by Carausius in his own hands. What prompted Allectus to destroy his master is not known, but perhaps some knowledge of the minister's cruelty or injustice towards the emperor's subjects had come to the ears of Carausius, and Allectus, fearing the result of an enquiry, made his position safe by direct action ; but the murder may have been simply the result of ambition, and similar to other happenings of the same kind in third-century history.

The coinage of Allectus is much more artistic and generally of better fabric than that of Carausius, barbarous and blundered coins being rare. His gold coins are of slightly greater average weight than those of his predecessor, and the bronze issues—there were none of silver—are more regular in style and compare favourably with the issues of the continental emperors. Also, Allectus struck an additional denomination, somewhat smaller than the antoninianus and about 60% of its weight, which, owing to the fact that the mint-mark almost always contains the letter Q in addition to the letters indicating the mint, has been classified as a quinarius.

The mints of Allectus were London and Colchester, and his coinage is here dealt with in similar manner to that of Carausius. Tables of obverse legends, obverse types and mint-marks are given, and it will be observed that none of these features present as much variation as in the coinage of Carausius.

Obverse legends.

1.	IMP C ALLECTVS P F I AVG.	8.	IMP C ALLECTVS P F AVGG
2.	IMP C ALLECTVS P F AVG	9.	IMP C ALLECTVS FELIX AVG
3.	IMP C ALLECTVS P AVG	10.	IMP C ALLECTVS AVG
4.	IMP C ALLECTVS P F IN OR INV AVG	11.	IMP ALLECTVS P F AVG
5.	IMP C ALLECTVS PIVS FELIX AVG	12.	ALLECTVS P F AVG
6.	IMP C ALLECTVS PIV or PI FEL AVG	13.	VIRTVS ALLECTI AVG
7.	IMP C ALLECTVS PI FE AVG	14.	IMP C ALLECTVS P F AV

Obverse types.

A. Radiate and draped bust of Allectus r.
AA. Radiate and draped bust l.
B. Laureate and draped bust r.
C. Radiate, draped and cuirassed bust r.
D. Laureate, draped and cuirassed bust r.
E. Laureate and cuirassed bust r.
F. Radiate and cuirassed bust r.
G. Radiate helmeted and cuirassed bust l., holding spear and shield.
H. Radiate and cuirassed bust l., with spear and shield.
J. Radiate and cuirassed bust l., holding sceptre surmounted by eagle.
K. Laur. head r.

A

K

Mint of London.   Mint-marks.

No.	Exergue	Left of Field	Right of Field	Remarks
1	A			
2	ML			
3	ML			
4	ML	D		
5	ML	S		
6	ML	S	A	
7	ML	S	B	
8	ML	S	C	
9	ML	S	F	
10	ML	S	M	
11	ML	S	P	
12	MSL			
13	MSL	S		
14	MSL	S	A	
15	MSL	S	P	
16	MLXX	S		
17	MLXX	S	P	
18	SML			
19	III	S	A	
20		D	.	
21		S	A	
22		S	P	
23			A	
24	QL			

Mint of Colchester.

No.	Exergue	Left of Field	Right of Field	Remarks
25				No letters in exergue or field
26	C			
27	C	S		
28	C	S	A	
29	C	S	P	
30	CL	S	A	
31	CL	S	P	
32	MC	S	A	
33	MSC			
34	PC			
35	QC			
36	SPC			
37		S	P	

Mint of London.

Æ aurei.

No.	Obv. Legend	Obv. Type	Reverse	Mint Mark	M. & S. Ref.
450	2	K	ADVENTVS AVG. Emperor on horseback l., raising r. hand : before horse, captive.	2	1
451	2	D	COMES AVG. Minerva l., with olive-branch and spear, leaning on shield.	2	2
452	2	D	COMES AVG. Victory adv. r., with wreath and palm.	2	3
453	2	B, D, E, or K	ORIENS AVG. Sol stdg. l., raising r. hand and holding globe, sometimes between two captives.	2 or 4	4
454	2	E	PAX AVG. Pax standing l., holding olive-branch and upright sceptre.	2 or 6	5

No.	Obv. Legend	Obv. Type	Reverse	Mint Mark	M. & S. Ref.
455	2	E	PAX AVG. Pax as above, but with transverse sceptre.	2	6
456	12	B or E	As preceding.	2	7
457	2	E	PAX AVG. Pax galloping l. in biga.	2	8
458	2	B or E	SALVS AVG. Salus stdg. r., feeding serpent held in her arms.	2	9
459	2	E	SPES AVG. Spes walking l., holding flower.	2	10
460	12	B	As preceding.	2	11
461	2	E	VICTORIA AVG. Victory adv. r., with wreath and palm; before her, captive.	1	12
462	1	E	VIRTVS AVG. Mars stdg. r., holding spear and leaning on shield.	12	13
463	2	E	VIRTVS AVG. Emperor galloping r., spearing fallen enemy.	20	14

The following piece, in the Bodleian Library collection, Oxford, may perhaps be classed as a denarius, as it is struck in very base white metal.

464 *Obv.* 3 E. ℞. SALVS AVG. Salus stdg. l., feeding serpent held in her arms. Mint-mark 3. *M. & S.* 15.

Æ antoniniani.

No.	Obv. Legend	Obv. Type	Reverse	Mint Mark	M. & S. Ref.
465	2	F	AEQVITAS AVG. Aequitas l., with scales and cornucopiae.	6	16
466	2	C	COMES AVG. As No. 451.	14	17
467	2	C or F	FELICITAS SEC. Felicitas l., with sceptre or caduceus and cornucopiae.	6	18
468	2	A	FORTVNA AVG. Fortuna seated l., holding rudder and cornucopiae: at foot, wheel.	2	19
469	2	F	HILARITAS AVG. Hilaritas l., with palm and cornucopiae.	6, 11, 14 or 15	20
470	2	F	IOVI CONSERVATORI. Jupiter l., with thunderbolt and sceptre.	6	21
471	2	A, C, F or H	LAETIT, LAETITI or LAETITIA AVG. Laetitia l., holding wreath and anchor (or baton).	2, 5, 6, 7, 11 or 14	22
472	1	F	LAETITIA AVG. As above, with wreath and baton.	14	23
473	2	F	LEG II. Lion walking l.	2	24
474	2	C or F	MONETA AVG. Moneta l., with scales and cornucopiae.	6 or 14	25
475	2	C or F	ORIENS AVG. Sol stdg. l., r. hand raised, l. holding globe.	6, 11 or 22	26
476	3	A	As preceding.	6	27
477	2	A, C, F or H	PAX AVG. As No. 454.	6, 11, 14, or 19	28
477a	1	A or F	As preceding. *Colln. of L. G. P. Messenger, Esq.*	11	—
478	5	F	As preceding.	11	29
479	14	A or F	As preceding.	16 or 17	30
480	13	G	As preceding.	6	31
481	1	A	PAX AVG. As No. 455.	6	32
482	2	A, C, F or H	As preceding.	6, 9, 10, 11, 14, 15 or 18	33
483	2	A or F	PIETAS AVG. Pietas l. before altar, holding patera.	6 or 14	34
484	2	A, C, F or J	PROVI. PROVID or PROVIDENTIA AVG. Providentia stdg. l., holding baton and cornucopiae; at her feet, globe.	6, 11 or 14	35

No.	OBV. LEGEND	OBV. TYPE	REVERSE	MINT MARK	M. & S. REF.
485	2	A, C, F or H	PROVID, PROVIT or PROVIDENTIA AVG. As preceding, but with globe and cornucopiae.	6, 11, 14 or 15	36
486	1	A OR F	PROVIDENTIA AVG. Type as No. 484.	6 or 14	37
487	2	A or F	PROVIDE OR PROVIDENTIA AVG. As above, but with sceptre in l.	6, 11 or 14	38
488	2	F	PROVID DEOR. As above, but with baton and cornucopiae.	11	39
489	2	F	ROMAE AETER. Roma l. in temple.	6	40
490	2	C	SAECVLI FELICITAS. Emperor r., with spear and globe.	11	41
491	2	A or F	SALVS AVG. As No. 458.	6, 11, 14 15 or 22	42
492	2	F	SALVS AVG. Salus stdg. l. by altar, with patera and sceptre.	6 or 8	43
493	2	A	SALVS AVG. Salus seated l., feeding serpent rising from altar.	6	44
494	2	C	SPES AVG. Spes walking l., holding flower.	6 or 11	45
495	2	F	SPES PVBLICA. As preceding.	6	46

496	2	F	TEMPOR or TEMPORVM FELICI or FELICITAS. Felicitas l., with caduceus and cornucopiae.	6, 11 or 14	47
497	2	A, C or F	VICTORIA AVG. Victory r. or l., with wreath and palm.	11	48
498	2	A, C or F	VIRTVS AVG. As No. 462.	6 or 11	49

499	2	A or F	,, ,, As No. 490.	6 or 10	50
500	2	F	,, ,, Hercules l., leaning on club.	6	51
501	2	C	,, ,, Hercules l. in temple, holding club.	2	52
502	2	A, C, or F	,, ,, Trophy between captives.	6	53
503	3	A	,, ,, As preceding.	23	54

Æ quinarii.

504	2	A, C or F	VIRTVS AVG. Galley r. or l.	24	55
505	2	H	,, ,, Galley l.	24	56
506	2	A	,, ,, Galley as above, with bird on mast.	24	57
507	2	F	,, ,, As No. 504, but with Victory stdg. l. on galley.	24	58
508	2	A	,, ,, As preceding, but with Neptune seated l. on galley, holding anchor.	24	59

Mint of Colchester.

Æ antoniniani.

No.	OBV. LEGEND	OBV. TYPE	REVERSE	MINT MARK	M. & S. REF.
509	1	F	ABVND AVG. Abundantia l., pouring fruits into modius.	29	60
510	2	C	ABVNDANT or ABVNDANTIA AVG. As preceding.	29	61
511	2	F	ADVENTVS AVG. As No. 450.	36	62
512	2	F	AEQVITAS AVG. As No. 465.	29	63
513	2	F	COMES AVG. As No. 451.	29	64
514	2	F	DIANAE REDVCI. Diana r., head l., holding bow and leading stag.	36	65
515	2	F	FELICITAS SAECVLI. Felicitas l. at altar, with patera and caduceus.	29	66
516	1 or 2	C	FIDES EXERCITVS. Four standards.	29	67-8
517	2	C or F	FIDES MILITV or MILITVM. Fides l., holding one or two standards.	25, 27, 29 or 31.	69
518	3	F	As preceding.	29	70
519	2	F	HILARITAS AVG. As No. 469.	29	71
520	1	F	IOVI CONSER. As No. 470.	29	72
521	7	F	As preceding.	29	73
522	2	F	IOVI CONSERVATORI. As preceding.	29	74
523	1	A or C	LAETIT AVG. As No. 471.	29	75
524	2	A or C	As preceding.	28 or 29	76
525	2	F	LAETITI AVG. As preceding.	29, 31 or 32	77
526	6	A	As preceding.	29	78
527	2	A, C or F	LAETITIA AVG. As preceding.	29 or 31	79
528	11	F	As preceding.	29	80
529	2	A	LAETITIA AVGVSTI. As preceding.	29	81
530	1	F	MONETA AVG. As No. 474.	29	82
531	2	C or F	As preceding.	29	83
532	2	F	ORIENS AVG. As No. 475.	29	84
533	1	A or C	PAX AVG. As No. 454.	29	85
534	2	C or F	As preceding.	29	86
535	3	AA or C	As preceding.	29	87
536	5	A	As preceding.	29	88
537	4	A	As preceding.	29	89
538	1	A or C	PAX AVG. As No. 455.	29 or 37	90
539	2	A, C or F	As preceding.	29	91
540	2	A	As preceding, but with globe in r. hand.	26	92
541	8	F	PAX AVGGG. As No. 454.	26	93
542	2	A or C	PROVID AVG. As No. 485.	29	94
543	3	A	As preceding.	29	95
544	1	F	PROVID AVG. As No. 484.	29	96
545	2	A, C or F	As preceding.	29	97
546	3	A or C	As preceding.	29	98
547	6	C	As preceding.	29	99
548	7	C	As preceding.	29	100
549	9	A	As preceding.	26	101
550	2	C	PROVID AVG. Providentia l., with globe and transverse sceptre.	29	102
551	2	A	PROVIDE AVG. As preceding.	29	103
552	1	F	PROVIDENTIA AVG. As preceding.	31	104
553	2	F	As preceding.	29 or 31	105
554	3	C or F	As preceding.	29	106
555	1	C or F	Legend as preceding, type as No. 485	29	107
556	2	A or F	As preceding.	29 or 31	108
557	3	F	As preceding.	29	109
558	1	F	Legend as preceding, type as No. 484	29	110
559	2	C or F	As preceding.	29 or 31	111
560	3	F	As preceding.	29	112

No.	OBV. LEGEND	OBV. TYPE	REVERSE	MINT MARK	M. & S. REF.
561	2	F	ROMAE AETERN. Type as No. 489.	33	113
562	2	C	SALVS AVG. Salus stdg. l., holding sceptre and feeding serpent rising from altar.	29	114
563	2	A or F	SPES PVBL, PVBLIC or PVBLICA. Type as No. 494.	29	115
564	4	C	As preceding.	29	116
565	2	C or F	TEMPORA or TEMPORVM FELIC, FELICI, FELICIT or FELICITAS. Type as No. 496.	29, 30 or 31	117
566	3	F	TEMPORVM FELICI. As preceding.	29	118
567	1	A	VICTORIA AVG. Type as No. 497.	29	119
568	2	C or F	VIRTVS AVG. Type as No. 462.	29	121
569	2	C	,, ,, Type as No. 490.	29	122
570	2	A	VIRTVS EXERCIT. Four standards.	36	123

Æ quinarii.

No.	OBV. LEGEND	OBV. TYPE	REVERSE	MINT MARK	M. & S. REF.
571	2	A or F	LAETITIA AVG. Galley r. or l.	35	124
572	3	A or F	As preceding.	35	125
573	10	F	As preceding.	35	126
574	7	F	As preceding.	34 or 35	127
575	2	A or F	VIRTVS AVG. Type as preceding.	26 or 35	128
576	10	F	As preceding.	35	129
577	3	F	As preceding, but with helmsman standing aft.	35	130
578	2	A	VIRTVS AVG. Neptune seated l. on galley, holding anchor.	35	131

The following antoninianus is without any mint-mark, and has bust in high relief, the beard being more pointed than usual.

No.	OBV. LEGEND	OBV. TYPE	REVERSE	MINT MARK	M. & S. REF.
579	2	A	VICTORIA AVG. Victory walking l., holding wreath and palm.	25	132

If the ancient authorities are to be trusted, Allectus was a hard master to his subjects, and perhaps some hint of their disaffection reached the ears of the central government. Certain it is that in 296, after long preparations, Constantius Chlorus had sufficient strength at sea to make another attempt at the re-conquest of Britain. It may be—though there is no mention of it in the records—that many of Carausius' men, loyal enough to their old master but unwilling to support his murderer, had transferred their allegiance to Constantius. In any case the latter was able to divide his fleet into two portions and attack the island by what we have come to know as a " pincer movement." The left wing, under Asclepiodotus, sailed from the estuary of the Seine and, eluding the ships of Allectus, made a landfall on the Hampshire coast. Asclepiodotus landed his forces, burnt his ships and marched inland. The right wing of the fleet, under Constantius, sailed a little later, and, reaching the Kentish coast at Rutupiae (Richborough), sailed round Kent and up the Thames.

Allectus, whose army was quartered near London, received tidings of the landing in Hampshire, and immediately set off to deal with the invasion. The ensuing battle is believed to have been fought in the heath country of Hampshire, and the result was the complete defeat of Allectus, the latter being killed in the struggle or in the rout that ensued. The survivors of Allectus' forces retreated to London, and at once began to plunder the town as a preliminary to dispersing; but the ships of Constantius arrived in time to save the situation. The troops were landed at once, and soon dealt with the disorderly rabble which represented the remainder of Allectus' army. Thus by a short campaign the first British empire was brought to an end, and the island restored to the rule of the central government. In commemoration of this event the following gold medallion was struck.

580 FL VAL CONSTANTIVS NOBIL CAES. Laureate, draped and cuirassed bust r.
℞. REDDITOR LVCIS AETERNAE. Constantius on horseback r., holding spear :
before him, female figure kneeling l. before a city gate : the letters LON below
her indicate that she is a personification of London. In the foreground, a galley
r., and in ex., PTR. *N medallion*, mint of Trier.

This fine piece, which formed part of the great treasure of Roman medallions,
coins and jewellery found at Beaurains, near Arras, in September, 1922, is one of
the most important of the smaller monuments of Roman Britain. A notable example

of the medallic art of the period, it illustrates Constantius' victory in a most comprehensive way. We see the conqueror approaching the city gates and being
welcomed by the city-goddess of London, the abbreviation LON being inserted os
that there shall be no doubt as to her identity : we see the galley and the troops
by whom the city was saved from destruction ; and the legend " Restorer of the
Eternal Light " acclaims Constantius as the man who brought back the blessings
of Roman civilization to a province from which they had been, for some years,
withheld.

Four other gold medallions from the same treasure may have reference to the
reconquest of Britain, and although to the present author this reference is doubtful
the pieces are described below : they are somewhat smaller than No. 580.

580A FL VAL CONSTANTIVS NOBILISSIMVS C. Head of Constantius, wearing the lion-skin
of Hercules r.
℞. PIETAS AVGG. Constantius standing r., being crowned by Victory standing
behind him, and raising with his r. hand kneeling female figure who holds spear
and oblong shield in her l. hand : in ex., PTR.
N medallion, dia. 33 mm. : mint of Trier.

580B FL VAL CONSTANTIVS NOB CAES. Laur. and dr. bust of Constantius r., holding
eagle-tipped sceptre.
℞. As preceding.

580C IMP ĐIOCLETIANVS PIVS FELIX AVG. Laur. head of Diocletian r.
℞. As preceding.

580D GAL VAL MAXIMIANVS NOB CAES. Laur., dr. and cuir. bust of Maximian r.
℞. As preceding.

The kneeling female figure who is being assisted to rise by Constantius has been
assumed by some students to represent Britain's restoration to the empire, but
there is nothing in the legend to suggest this, and the reference to Britain may be
taken as " non proven." The five medallions are in the French national collection.

Chapter VIII : The Mint of London under the Tetrarchy.

Before dealing with this section of the coinage, it may be well to remind the reader of the sweeping re-organisation of the Roman Empire carried out by Diocletian. Raised to the purple by his troops in 284, he found the affairs of the state both chaotic and corrupt, and he realised that one of the chief causes of trouble was the uncertainty of succession to the throne. All through the third century there had almost always been civil war, threatened or actual, when an emperor died, and from the death of Severus in 211 to that of Carinus in 285 no emperor had reigned more than fifteen years. Most of them, indeed, had much shorter reigns, and almost all of them came to violent ends. Diocletian, soon after his becoming emperor, associated with himself as joint ruler the general Maximianus, and it was arranged that each should appoint an heir-designate with the rank of Caesar. Thus there would be two Augusti and two Caesars to watch over the welfare of the empire; and the plan was that the Augusti should abdicate after twenty years of rule, the two Caesars to become Augusti in their places : the latter would then appoint or adopt two new Caesars so as to secure the succession and avoid any civil war that might otherwise ensue. From the virtual division of the empire into four parts, we know this scheme as the Tetrarchy. Excellent as the plan was, it did not take into account the factor of human ambition, and we can now consider what actually happened.

Diocletian and Maximianus having divided the empire between them, ruling as equals except that Diocletian always asserted himself as the senior, the two Caesars were duly appointed in 293. Diocletian, whose particular sphere was the eastern portion of the empire, appointed a soldier of high rank, Galerius, as Caesar, and gave him charge of the Danubian provinces and the Balkans. The emperor later adopted Galerius into his family and gave him his daughter Valeria in marriage. Maximianus, who ruled the western portion with Milan as his capital, appointed Constantius, known as " Chlorus " (that is, " the pale ") as his assistant with the rank of Caesar. Constantius governed the western provinces—Spain, Gaul and, later, Britain—from Trier, and we have seen with what energy and success he campaigned against Allectus : of his further actions in Britain we shall hear more later.

In 305 Diocletian abdicated after his twenty years of rule and compelled Maximianus, who was somewhat unwilling to relinquish his high status, to do likewise. Galerius and Constantius were at once raised to the rank of Augustus, and two new Caesars were appointed. Galerius, perhaps unwisely, conferred the rank on his nephew Maximinus Daza or Daia, giving him the government of Syria and Egypt, and also appointed Flavius Severus (usually known to us as Severus II to distinguish him from Septimius Severus) to be Caesar and assistant to Constantius. Thus far the Diocletianic scheme had been carried out almost as arranged ; but when Constantius died at York in 306 his son Constantine (later " the Great ") immediately assumed the rank of Caesar and a few months later was saluted by his troops as Augustus, and the empire was once more disturbed by the threat of civil strife. Galerius, incensed at the violation of the system as laid down, was yet unwilling to have recourse to arms, and agreed to accept Constantine as a Caesar provided that Severus should succeed as Augustus in the west. Constantine, however, refused to be less than Augustus, and the situation was further complicated by

Maxentius, the son of Maximianus who had been passed over for any promotion on account of his dissolute and indolent habits, taking part in a conspiracy against the ruling emperors and himself being hailed Augustus on Oct. 28th, 306.   His father Maximianus seized the opportunity of emerging from his enforced retirement and taking part in the revolt.   Thus in 306 the rank of Augustus was claimed by five men, Galerius and Severus, the lawful holders of the title, and also Maximianus, Constantine and Maxentius.

It may be appropriate at this point briefly to outline the history of the next few years.   Severus was instructed by Galerius to deal with the rebellious Maxentius, who had seized and held Italy and part of Africa, but in the ensuing campaign Severus was defeated and captured, and subsequently compelled to commit suicide (307).   Galerius then appointed Licinius, for many years his friend and comrade, as Augustus and co-emperor.   Maximinus Daza, who had himself expected to be elected Augustus, was extremely indignant at having been passed over, and assumed the coveted rank without authority, afterwards obtaining, not without difficulty, Galerius' agreement to the step.   Thus in 307 there were no less than six Augusti: Galerius, Licinius, Constantine, Maximinus Daza, Maxentius and old Maximianus, and the Diocletianic system had to all intents and purposes broken down.

The subsequent fate of the persons may be dealt with here, although it involves some anticipation of our story.   Galerius, after a troubled reign, died of disease in 311.   Maximianus was again compelled to abdicate in 308, and two years later, being implicated in a plot against Constantine, was ordered to end his own life.   Thus in 311 only four of the six Augusti remained, Constantine and Maxentius in the west and Licinius and Maximinus Daza in the east.   In 312 Constantine, who ruled Gaul, Britain and Spain and was extremely popular with his subjects, decided to put an end to the usurpation of Maxentius, and accordingly crossed the Alps at the head of a large army.   After successes in the north of Italy he defeated Maxentius at the battle of the Milvian Bridge, Maxentius himself being drowned in the Tiber along with many of his fleeing soldiers.

Licinius, who had been given the Illyrian provinces in 307, had agreed to divide the eastern portion of the empire with Maximinus Daza, who ruled Syria and Egypt. Licinius, however, feared the ambition of his colleague, and accordingly allied himself to Constantine, whose sister Constantia he married.   When Maximinus did at length break his agreement with Licinius and invade his territory (313), the armies of the two contestants met near Adrianople, and Maximinus was defeated : he fled to Tarsus, and soon afterwards died.   The number of Augusti was thus reduced to two, and for some years it seemed that the Diocletianic division between East and West had been established once more, for although war had broken out between Constantine and Licinius in 314, peace was soon made.   It was not until 323 that the final conflict began, and in this Constantine was completely victorious. After a battle fought near Scutari Licinius was taken prisoner, and soon afterwards was put to death.   Thus by 324 the system of Diocletian was definitely at an end, and after thirty-eight years the whole Roman Empire was once more ruled by one man.

These historical details have been given because when the coins of the London mint under the Tetrarchy are listed they will be found to include pieces issued in the names of Maximinus Daza and Licinius, who had no connection with the West at all.   Apparently it was part of the standard policy of the imperial mints that all ruling Augusti and Caesars should be commemorated on the coinage, regardless of where the mints might be situated within the empire.   Neither Maximinus nor Licinius can have had any authority over the London mint, as their provinces were far away, but large issues of coins seem to have been made bearing their names.

It may be noted here that the coins of Constantine as Caesar will be dealt with in this work as part of the general series of Constantinian issues : this is being done for ease in classification.

We can now return to the condition of Britain at the time of the defeat of Allectus. Constantius found the country in a very disturbed state, and set about the task of re-construction with characteristic vigour. The Wall and its associated works were ruinous, partly from neglect and partly from damage by the northern invaders or rebels. Constantius carried out vast schemes of re-building, and the frontier defences were restored, as was the legionary fortress of York. Other towns in the more civilised parts of Britain received his attention, and possibly the bastions were added to London Wall in his time. The chief monuments of his period, however, are the great coastal forts of the Saxon Shore, which form a chain of defence from the Wash to the Isle of Wight. These were founded to counter the menace of Frankish and Saxon pirates, and as they have been dated by excavation to the late third century there seems little doubt that they were the work of Constantius. The forts concerned are as follows :—

Branodunum : Brancaster, on the north Norfolk coast.

Garianonum : Burgh Castle, on the river Waveney in Suffolk.

Walton Castle, once standing not far from Felixstowe, but now entirely destroyed through erosion by the sea.

Othona : Bradwell-juxta-Mare, not far from the estuary of the river Blackwater, in Essex.

Regulbium : Reculver, on the north coast of Kent.

Rutupiae : Richborough, close to Sandwich, Kent.

Dubris or Portus Dubris : Dover.

Portus Lemanus : Lympne, on the inland edge of Romney Marsh, Kent.

Anderida : Pevensey, in Sussex.

Portus Adurni : Porchester, at the head of Portsmouth Harbour.

To these may be added a possible fort at Carisbrooke, Isle of Wight, and also certain of the defences on the west coast such as those at Carnarvon and Cardiff. The latter were not intended to deal with the incursions of Saxons, but with raids from Ireland which began about this time to be a menace to the peace and security of western Britain.

These coastal forts lie mainly on harbours and were evidently intended to be fortified bases for squadrons of warships, and the remains that survive show them to have been places of exceptional strength. Some of them have been deserted by the sea since Roman times, and the surviving works at, for instance, Lympne and Pevensey are far from any navigable water. Even Richborough, which was a fort and harbour of considerable importance from the early days of the Roman occupation, is now more than two miles inland and is separated from the sea by marshes and sandy flats. Porchester, however, is still washed by the waters of Portsmouth Harbour, and, despite the Norman castle and other buildings which have been erected within it, still gives us the best idea of the grand scale on which this series of defences was conceived.

Certain changes in the internal administration of Britain were also made about this time. The country had been divided into two provinces by Severus, and these were now increased to four. Britain became one of the twelve " dioceses " of the empire, and was governed by a *vicarius*, an official subordinate to the praetorian prefect of Gaul. Regarding military affairs, we find three new officers created : the *Dux Britanniarum*, in charge of the frontier zone with headquarters at York ; the *Comes Litoris Saxonici*, who commanded the Saxon shore forts mentioned above ; and the *Comes Britanniarum* with a field army. But the latter position was probably instituted some years later, perhaps after 368.

It is probable that the transfer of the Second Legion from Caerleon to Rich-borough was ordered by Constantius, in an attempt to man the chief of his new forts with the best available troops. The other legions, the Twentieth at Chester and the Sixth at York, could not be moved without endangering the northern part of the province.

In the lists of coins which follow, only the mint of London is concerned, as the " C " mint, whether Camulodunum or Clausentum, was closed on the defeat of Allectus, and never re-opened.

The only denomination issued by the London mint during the period under consideration was the *follis*, one of the new coins introduced by Diocletian in his reform of the coinage in 296. The *follis* is a bronze coin, and some specimens show traces of silvering, but whether all were originally silver-washed is a matter that has not yet been decided. Early specimens of the *follis* are about 28 mm. in diameter, but the coin declined in size and weight until, at the end of the Tetrarchy, the diameter was 20 mm. or even less. The commonest reverse is that illus-

trated here, the legend being GENIO POPVLI ROMANI and the type the Genius of the Roman People standing to left, holding a patera and cornucopiae and crowned with a *modius* or corn-measure. Early *folles* of the London mint bear no mint-mark, but their style is unmistakeable, some of the laureate and cuirassed busts bearing a strong resemblance to those on coins of Carausius.

In the following lists, where no mint-mark is given, the exergue may be taken as being plain, and where the legends GENIO POPVLI ROMANI or GENIO POP ROM occur, the type is as illustrated above unless otherwise noted.

Diocletian.

Before abdication in 305.

581 IMP DIOCLETIANVS AVG. Laureate and cuirassed bust of Diocletian r.
R. GENIO POPVLI ROMANI. *Cohen* 87.

582 IMP DIOCLETIANVS AVG. Laureate and cuirassed bust l., with spear and shield.
R. GENIO POPVLI ROMANI. *C.* 90.

583 IMP DIOCLETIANVS P AVG. Laur. and cuir. bust r.
R. GENIO POPVLI ROMANI. *C.* 91.

584 IMP DIOCLETIANVS P F AVG. Laur. and cuir. bust r.
R. GENIO POPVLI ROMANI. *C.* 93.

585 IMP DIOCLETIANVS P P AVG. Laur. and cuir. bust r.
R. GENIO POPVLI ROMANI. *C.* 93 *var. Ashmolean Museum.*

586 IMP C DIOCLETIANVS P F AVG. Laur. head r.
R. GENIO POPVLI ROMANI. *C.* 101.

587 As preceding, with LON in exergue. *C.* 101. *Ashmolean Museum.*

588 As preceding, with LN in ex. *C.* 101. *British Museum.*

589 As preceding, with PLN in ex. *C.* 101. *In the collection of the late R. Cyril Lockett, Esq.*

590 IMP C DIOCLETIANVS P F AVG. Laur. and cuir. bust r.
R. GENIO POPVLI ROMANI. *C.* 103.

After abdication, 305-307.

591 D N DIOCLETIANO P F S AVG. Laureate bust r., wearing imperial mantle and holding branch.
R. GENIO POP ROM. Female figure standing l., holding branch downwards and sceptre : in ex., PLN. *C.* 83.

592 D N DIOCLETIANO FELICISSMO SEN AVG. Type as preceding.
R. PROVIDENTIA DEORVM QVIES AVGG. Female figure standing r., extending r.
hand : facing her, Providentia standing l., holding branch upwards and sceptre.
C. 423.

593 As preceding, but Providentia holds her branch downwards. C. 426.

594 D N DIOCLETIANO BAEATISSIMO SEN AVG. Type as preceding.
R. As preceding. C. 425.

595 D N DIOCLETIANO P F S AVG. Type as preceding.
R. QVIES AVGG. Female figure (? Repose) standing l., holding branch and sceptre.
C. 428.

596 As preceding, with PLN in ex. C. 428.

Maximianus I, Herculeus.

Before abdication in 305.

597 IMP MAXIMIANVS AVG. Laur. and cuir. bust of Maximian r.
R. GENIO POPVLI ROMANI. C. 153.

598 IMP MAXIMIANVS AG. Laur. head r.
R. GENIO POPVLI ROMANI. C. 153 var. *Ashmolean Museum.*

599 IMP MAXIMIANVS AVG. Laur. and cuir. bust l., with spear and shield.
R. GENIO POPVLI ROMANI. Cf. C. 154.

600 IMP MAXIMIANVS P AVG. Laur. and cuir. bust r.
R. GENIO POPVLI ROMANI. C. 156.

601 IMP MAXIMIANVS P F AVG. Laur. head r.
R. GENIO POPVLI ROMANI. In ex., LN. C. 159. *Ashmolean Museum.*

602 IMP MAXIMIANVS P F AVG. Laur. and cuir. bust r.
R. GENIO POPVLI ROMANI. C. 162.

603 As preceding, but bust laur., draped and cuirassed. C. 162.

604 IMP MAXIMIANVS P F AVG. Laur. and cuir. bust l., with spear and shield.
R. GENIO POPVLI ROMANI. Cf. C. 163.

604a As preceding, but laur. bust l., with lion's skin on l. shoulder and club on r.

605 IMP C MAXIMIANVS P F AVG. Laur. head r.
R. GENIO POPVLI ROMANI. C. 179.

606 As preceding, with LON in ex. C. 179.

607 IMP C MAXIMIANVS P F AVG. Laur. and cuir. bust r.
R. GENIO POPVLI ROMANI. C. 180.

608 IMP C MAXIMIANVS P P AVG. Laur. and cuir. bust r.
R. GENIO POPVLI ROMANI. C. 180 var. *Ashmolean Museum.*

609 IMP MAXIMIANVS PI FE AVG. Laur. head r.
R. GENIO POPVLI ROMANI. In ex., LON. C.—. *British Museum.*

610 IMP C MAXIMIANVS P FFL AVG. Laur. and cuir. bust r.
R. GENIO POPVLI ROMANI. C.—. *British Museum.*

611 IMP C MAXIMIANIVS P F AVG. Laur. and cuir. bust r., with spear and shield.
R. GENIO POPVLI ROMANI. C. 181 var.

After abdication, 305-308.

612 D N MAXIMIANO P F S AVG. Laur. and cuir. bust r.
R. GENIO POP ROM. Usual type except that Genius sometimes wears a turreted head-dress instead of modius : in ex., PLN. *C.* 142 (turreted) ; *C.* 147 (modius).

613 IMP MAXIMIANVS P F AVG. Laur. and cuir. bust r.
R. GENIO POP ROM. In ex., PLN. *C.* 143.

614 D N MAXIMIANO P F S AVG. Laur. and cuir. bust r.
R. HERCVLI CONSERVATORI. Hercules standing facing, head l., resting r. hand on club and in l. holding bow : in ex., PLN. *C.* 251.

615 D N MAXIMIANO P F S AVG. Laur. and cuir. bust r.
R. MARS VICTOR. Mars advancing r., holding spear and trophy : in ex., PLN. *C.* 389.

616 D N MAXIMIANO P F S AVG. Laur. and cuir. bust r.
R. MARTI PATRI PROPVGNATORI. Mars adv. r., with spear and shield : in ex., PLN. *C.*—. *Ashmolean Museum.*

617 D N MAXIMIANO BAEATISSIMO SEN AVG. Laur. bust r., wearing imperial mantle and holding branch.
R. PROVIDENTIA DEORVM QVIES AVGG. Type similar to No. 592. *C.* 490.

618 As preceding, but type as No. 593. *C.* 491.

619 D N MAXIMIANO FELICISSIMO SEN AVG. Type as preceding.
R. As preceding. *C.* 493.

620 D N MAXIMIANO P F S AVG. Laur. and cuir. bust r.
R. ROMAE AETER. Roma seated facing, head l., within hexastyle temple : in ex., PLN. *C.* 501.

Constantius I, Chlorus.

As Caesar, 293-305.

621 CONSTANTIVS NOB CAES. Laur. head of Constantius r.
R. GENIO POPVLI ROMANI. *C.* 61.

622 CONSTANTIVS NOB CAES. Laur. and cuir. bust r., with spear and shield.
R. GENIO POPVLI ROMANI. In field l., B : in ex., PLN. *C.* 63. *In the collection of the late R. Cyril Lockett, Esq.*

623 CONSTANTIVS NOB C. Laur. head r.
R. GENIO POPVLI ROMANI. *C.* 71.

624 As preceding, but with laur. and cuir. bust r. *C.* 72.

625 As preceding, but with laur. and cuir. bust l., with spear and shield. *C.* 73.

626 CONSTANTIVS NOBIL C. Laur. and cuir. bust r.
R. GENIO POPVLI ROMANI. *C.* 77.

627 FL VAL CONSTANTIVS NOB C. Laur. head r.
R. GENIO POPVLI ROMANI. *C.* 83.

628 As preceding, but with LON in ex. *C.* 83. *British Museum.*

629 FL VAL CONSTANTIVS NOB C. Laur. and cuir. bust r.
R̵. GENIO POPVLI ROMANI. *C.* 84.

As Augustus, 305-306.

630 IMP CONSTANTIVS AVG. Laur. and cuir. bust r.
R̵. GENIO POPVLI ROMANI. *C.* 93.

631 As preceding, but with IMP CONSTANTIVS P AVG. *C.* 94.

632 As preceding, but with IMP CONSTANTIVS P F AVG. *C.* 95.

633 As preceding, but with IMP CONSTANTIVS PI FEL AVG. *C.* 96.

634 As preceding, but with IMP CONSTANTIVS P FEL AVG. *C.* 96 *var.*

635 As preceding, but with IMP CONSTANTIVS PIVS F AVG. *C.* 97.

636 As preceding, but with IMP CONSTANTIVS PIVS FEL AVG. *C.* 98.

637 As preceding, but with IMP CONSTANTIVS P FELIX AVG. *C.* 99.

After death in 306 A.D.

638 DIVO CONSTANTIO PIO. Laur., veiled and cuir. bust r.
R̵. MEMORIA FELIX. Altar, lit, between two eagles facing : in ex., PLN. *C.* 179.

Galerius.

As Caesar, 293-305.

639 MAXIMIANVS NOB C. Laur. and cuir. bust of Galerius r.
R̵. GENIO POPVLI ROMANI. *C.* 54.

640 MAXIMIANVS NOB CAES. Laur. head r.
R̵. GENIO POPVLI ROMANI. *C.* 56.

641 As preceding, but with laur., dr. and cuir. bust r. *C.* 57.

642 MAXIMIANVS NOB CAES. Laur., dr. and cuir. bust l., holding eagle-tipped sceptre.
C. 61 *var.* *British Museum.*

643 MAXIMIANVS NOBIL C. Laur. and cuir. bust r.
R̵. GENIO POPVLI ROMANI. *C.* 65.

644 MAXIMIANVS NOBIL CAES. Laur., dr. and cuir. bust r.
℞. GENIO POPVLI ROMANI. *C.* 69 *var.* *Ashmolean Museum.*
645 G VAL MAXIMIANVS NOB C. Laur. head r.
℞. GENIO POPVLI ROMANI. *C.* 74.

646 As preceding, but with LON in ex. *C.* 74.
647 As No. 645, but with laur. and cuir. bust r. *C.* 74 *var.* *Ashmolean Museum.*

As Augustus, 305-311.

N.B.—*Nos. 648, 649, 651, 653 and 655 resemble, as to types and legends, Nos. 602, 603, 607, 610 and 613 respectively of Maximianus I, but can be distinguished by portrait and general style.*

648 IMP MAXIMIANVS P F AVG. Laur. and cuir. bust r.
℞. GENIO POPVLI ROMANI. *C.*—. *British Museum.*
649 As preceding, but with laur., dr. and cuir. bust r. *C.*—. *British Museum.*
650 IMP C MAXIMIANVS P F AVG. Otherwise as preceding. *C.*—. *B.M.*
651 As preceding, but with laur. and cuir. bust r. *C.*—. *B.M.*
652 As preceding, but with IMP MAXIMIANVS P F IN AVG. *C.*—. *B.M.*
653 As preceding, but with IMP C MAXIMIANVS P FEL AVG. *C.*—. *B.M.*
654 As preceding, but with IMP C MAXIMIANVS PIVS FEL AVG. *C.*—. *B.M.*

655 IMP MAXIMIANVS P F AVG. Laur. and cuir. bust r.
℞. GENIO POP ROM. *C.*—. *British Museum.*
656 As preceding, with PLN in ex. *C.*—. *Ashmolean Museum.*
657 IMP C MAXIMIANVS P F AVG. Otherwise as preceding. *C.*—.

Severus II.

As Caesar, 305-306.
658 SEVERVS NOBILIS C. Laur. dr. and cuir. bust of Severus r.
℞. GENIO POPVLI ROMANI. *C.* 21.
659 As preceding, but with SEVERVS NOBILISSIM C. *C.* 22.
660 As preceding, but with SEVERVS NOBILISSIMVS C. *C.* 23.

661 As preceding, but with SEVERVS NOBILISSIMVS CAES. *C.* 24.
662 As preceding, but with SEVERVS NOBILISSIMVS CAESAR. *C.* 25.

As Augustus, 306-307.

663 IMP C SEVERVS PIVS FEL AVG. Laur., dr. and cuir. bust r.
R. GENIO POPVLI ROMANI. *C.* 35.
664 IMP SEVERVS P F AVG. Laur. and cuir. bust r.
R. GENIO POPVLI ROMANI. *C.* 40 *var.*

Maximinus II, Daza.

As Caesar, 305-307.

665 MAXIMINVS NOBIL C. Helmeted and cuir. bust of Maximinus r., with spear and shield.
R. GENIO POPVLI ROMANI. *C.* 74.
666 MAXIMINVS NOBILIS C. Laur., dr. and cuir. bust r.
R. GENIO POPVLI ROMANI. *C.* 75.
667 MAXIMINVS NOB CAES. Laur. and cuir. bust r.
R. GENIO POPVLI ROMANI. *C.* 76.
668 MAXIMINVS NOBILI CAES. Laur., dr. and cuir. bust r.
R. GENIO POPVLI ROMANI. *C.* 77.
669 MAXIMINVS NOBILISSIMVS CAES. Similar type.
R. GENIO POPVLI ROMANI. *C.* 79.
669a As preceding, with C instead of CAES. *C.* 79 *var.*
670 MAXIMINVS NOBILISSIMVS CAESAR. Similar type.
R. GENIO POPVLI ROMANI. *C.*—. *British Museum.*
671 GAL VAL MAXIMINVS NOB C. Similar type.
R. GENIO POPVLI ROMANI. *C.* 83 *var.*
672 GAL VAL MAXIMINVS NOBILI C. Similar type.
R. GENIO POPVLI ROMANI. *C.* 83 *var.*
673 GAL VAL MAXIMINVS NOB C. Similar type.
R. GENIO POP ROM. In ex., PLN. *C.* 56.
674 As preceding, but with laur. and dr. bust r. *C.* 57.
675 As No. 673, but genius wears turreted crown instead of modius. *C.* 66.

As Augustus, 307-314.

676 IMP MAXIMINVS P F AVG. Laur. and cuir. bust r.
R. COMITI AAVVGG. Sol standing l., holding globe and whip : in field, r., star : in ex., PLN. *C.* 5.
677 *Obv.* as preceding.
R. COMITI AAVVGG. Sol standing l., head r., raising r. hand and holding whip : in field, l., star : in ex., PLN. *C.* 5 *var.*
678 *Obv.* as preceding.
R. GENIO POP ROM. Genius wears turreted crown : in ex., PLN. *C.* 69.
679 As preceding, with star in l. of *rev.* field. *C.* 69.
680 As preceding, but with star in r. of *rev.* field. *C.* 69.
681 As preceding, but with star and T in l. of *rev.* field, and star and F in r. *C.* 69. *British Museum.*
682 IMP MAXIMINVS P AVG. Otherwise as No. 680. *C.* 72.
683 IMP MAXIMINVS P F AVG. Laur. and cuir. bust r.
R. MARTI CONSERVATORI. Mars standing r., holding spear and leaning on shield : in field, l., star and ꟼ : in field, r., star and T : in ex., PLN. *C.* 131 *var. British Museum.*

Licinius I. 307-324.

684 IMP LICINIVS P F AVG. Laur. and cuir. bust of Licinius r.
R. COMITI AAVVGG. Sol standing l., holding globe and whip : in field r., star : in ex., PLN. *C.* 3.
685 *Obv.* as preceding.
R. GENIO POP ROM : in field, S F : in ex., MLL. *C.* 49 (modius) or 53 (turreted).
686 As preceding, but in ex., MSL. *C.* 49 or 53.

687 As preceding, but in field r., star : in ex., P L N.   *C.* 49 or 53.

688 As preceding, but star in l. of field.   *C.* 49 or 53.

689 As preceding, but in field, S.F.   *C.* 49 or 53.

690 Similar, but *obv.* type to l., and star in l. of *rev.* field.   *C.*—.

691 IMP LICINIVS P AVG.   Laur. and cuir. bust r.
R. Type as preceding : in field S P ; in ex., MLN.   *C.*—.

692 *Obv.* as preceding.
R. SECVRITAS AVGG.   Securitas standing l., r. hand on head, leaning on pillar :
in field, l., star : in ex., PLN.   *C.* 154.

693 *Obv.* as preceding.
R. SOLI INVICTO COMITI.   Sol standing l., raising r. hand and holding globe : in
field, SF : in ex., MLN.   *C.* 161.

694 IMP LICINIVS P F AVG.   Laur., dr. and cuir. bust r.
R. As preceding, but in field S P and in ex., MLN.   *C.* 163.

695 As preceding, but in ex., MSL.   *C.* 163.

696 IMP LICINIVS P F AVG.   Laur. and cuir. bust r., otherwise as preceding.   *C.* 163.

697 As preceding, but S F in *rev.* field.   *C.* 163.

698 As preceding, but in *rev.* field T F and in ex., PLN.   *C.* 163.

699 *Obv.* as preceding.
R. SOLI INVICTO COMITI.   Sol in quadriga facing, head l., raising r. hand and
holding globe and whip : in field S P, in ex., MSL.   *C.* 164.

700 *Obv.* as preceding.
R. VICTORIAE LAETAE PRINC PERP.   Two Victories placing a shield inscr. VOT PR
on altar : in ex., two captives seated back to back between the letters P and L.   *C.* 177.

701 IMP LICINIVS AVG.   Laur. and cuir. bust r.
R. as preceding.   *C.* 174.

702 As preceding, but without P and L in ex.   *C.* 176.

———❖———

Chapter IX. The House of Constantine.

The coinage of the mint of London for this emperor and his family is so extensive and exhibits so great a variety of legends, types, and mint-marks, that it has been thought more convenient to reduce it to tabular form. Accordingly, the following system of references to obverse types and mint-marks will be used throughout the whole series, with the exception of the coins of Helena and Fausta which will be fully described in their proper place.

Obverse types.

A   Laureate head r.
B   Laur. and cuirassed bust r.
C   Laur., draped and cuir. bust r.
D   Helmeted and cuir. bust r.
E   Helmeted, laur. and cuir. bust r.
F   Laur. and cuir. bust r., holding eagle-tipped sceptre.
G   Laur. and cuir. bust r., with spear and shield.
H   Helmeted and cuir. bust r., with spear and shield.
J   Helmeted, laur. and cuir. bust r., holding globe surmounted by figure of Victory
K   Helmeted, laur. and cuir. bust r., with spear and shield.
L   Helmeted, radiate and cuir. bust r., with spear and shield.
M   Laur. bust r., wearing imperial mantle, holding eagle-tipped sceptre.
N   Helmeted, dr. and cuir. bust r., holding globe surmounted by figure of Victory.
O   Laur. and dr. bust r., wearing imperial mantle.
P   Radiate and draped bust r.
R   Radiate and cuirassed bust r.
S   Radiate, draped and cuirassed bust r.
T   Radiate and cuirassed bust, holding eagle-tipped sceptre.

The above types are all to right ; but if the index letter is doubled, a bust to left is indicated.

Mint-marks.

The mint-marks of this period are as follows, London being, of course, the only mint :

No.	Exergue	Left of Field	Right of Field	
1	PLN			
2	PLN	‿		
3	PLN	★		
4	PLN		★	
5	PLN	‿	★	
6	PLN	S	F	
7	PLN	S	P	
8	PLN	T	F	
9	MLL	S	F	
10	MLN	S	F	
11	MLN	S	P	
12	MSL	S	F	
13	MSL	S	P	
14	P LON			
15	P LON ‿			
16	P LON	F	B	
17	Two captives seated back to back between P and L.			
18	The same, without the letters.			
19	LON			
20	PLON	P	A	

The description of the reverse types should be sufficient for identification, but one point may be noted. In coins with the legends GENIO POPVLI ROMANI and GENIO POP ROM, it is sometimes difficult to tell whether the Genius is wearing a modius or a turreted crown.

The details of this section of the coinage have been based on M. Jules Maurice's paper "L'atelier monetaire de Londres (Londinium) pendant la periode Constantinienne," which appeared in the *Numismatic Chronicle*, 3rd Series, Vol. XX, 1899, and the translation and tabulation into the following form are almost entirely the work of Mr. Allan P. Pallett, whose co-operation is gratefully acknowledged.

Maurice divided the various issues of the mint into seven periods, as follows :—

    I.   July 306—May 309.
   II. May 309—June 313.
  III. 314.
  IV. Jan. 315—March 317.
   V. March 317—320.
  VI. 320-Nov. 324.
 VII. Nov. 324—Sept. 326.

In the following tables, the column headed " M " shows the period to which Maurice allocated the various coins. Denominations have not been given, as although the earliest pieces are certainly *folles* of full size, the series exhibits a gradual decrease in size and weight until those of the later periods are the small " third brass " so characteristic of the time.

The column headed " C " is the reference to Cohen : a coin " not in Cohen " will be indicated by N.

Constantine the Great
(*Caesar*, 306-308, *Augustus*, 308-337 A.D.).

Obverse Legends :—

  1 CONSTANTINVS AG
  2 CONSTANTINVS AVG
  3 CONSTANTINVS P AG
  4 CONSTANTINVS P AVG
  5 CONSTANTINVS P F AVG
  6 CONSTANTINVS MAX AVG   6A CONSTANTINVS MAX AG
  7 FL VAL CONSTANTINVS NOB C
  8 IMP CONSTANTINVS AG
  9 IMP CONSTANTINVS AVG
 10 IMP CONSTANTINVS MAX AVG   10A IMP CONSTANTINVS MAX AG
 11 IMP CONSTANTINVS P AVG
 12 IMP CONSTANTINVS P F AVG

No.	Obv. Legend	Obv. Type	Reverse	Mint Mark	M	C
703	5	HH	ADVENTVS AVG. Emperor on horseback l., with spear : before him, captive.	4	II	1
704	4	KK	As preceding.	4	II	2
705	4	DD	,,	4	II	2 v.
706	4	GG	,,	4	II	N
707	5	B	,,	4	II	3
708	5	HH	ADVENTVS AVG N. Type as preceding.	4	II	6
709	5	B	As preceding.	4	II	7
710	4	B	,,	4	II	8

No.	OBV. LEGEND	OBV. TYPE	REVERSE	MINT MARK	M	C
711	9	B	As preceding, without captive.	6	IV	N
712	9	HH	,,	6	IV	9
713	9	B	,,	9	IV	N
714	4	LL	ADVENTVS AVGG NN. Type as preceding.	4	II	N
715	2	F or M	BEATA TRANQVILLITAS. Altar inscr. VOTIS XX, surmounted by a globe and three stars.	14	VI	17
716	2	MM or TT	As preceding.	14	VI	18
717	2	DD	BEAT TRANQLITAS. Type as preceding.	14	VI	26
717a	1	DD	Type as preceding.	16	VI	N
718	1 or 2	D	,,	14	VI	N
719	2	FF	,,	14	VI	28
720	2	F	,,	14	VI	29
721	2	FF	,,	16	VI	28
722	1	F	,,	16	VI	30
723	4	B	CLARITAS REIPVBLICAE. Sol stdg. l., holding globe.	7	V	36
724	5	B	As preceding.	7	V	37
725	5	B	,,	5	V	37
726	4	GG	COMITI AVGG NN. Sol l., holding globe and whip.	4	II	40
727	4	KK	As preceding.	4	II	41
728	4	JJ	,,	4	II	N
729	4	NN	,,	4	II	42
730	1 or 4	B	,,	4	II	43
731	3	FF	,,	4	II	44
732	5	KK	,,	4	II	45/6
733	5	B	,,	4	II	48
734	1	GG	,,	4	II	50
735	2	FF	,,	4	II	N
736	2	HH	,,	4	II	49
737	5	B	COMITI AAVVGG. Type as preceding.	4	II	54
738	5	B	CONCORD MILIT. Concordia stg. l., holding two standards.	4	II	56
739	5	KK	As preceding.	4	II	N
740	2	KK	,,	4	II	57
741	4	B	,,	4	II	60
742	4	KK	,,	4	II	61
743	3	FF	,,	4	II	N
744	2	HH	CONCORDIA MILITVM. Type as preceding.	4	II	69
745	5	A	CONSTANTINI AVG around VOTIS XX in three lines.	1	VI	84
746	4	B	FELICITAS AVGG NN. Felicitas seated l., with branch and globe.	3	II	143
747	5	B	As preceding.	3	II	144
748	5	HH	,,	3	II	N
749	7	B	GENIO POP ROM. Genius stdg. l., crowned with modius, holding patera and cornucopiae.	1	I	N
750	11	B	As preceding.	1	I	204
751	7	B or C	GENIO POP ROM. Type as preceding, but Genius wears turreted crown.	1	I	196
751a	7	B	As preceding.	None	I	196
752	12	B	As preceding.	1	I	199
753	11	B	,,	1	I	N
754	12	B	,,	3	II	N
755	11	B	,,	4	II	N
756	12	B	,,	9	IV	N
757	12	B	,,	6	IV	N
758	9	B	,,	11	IV	N
759	4	B	,,	11	IV	209
760	3	BB	,,	13	IV	210 var.

No.	Obv. Legend	Obv. Type	Reverse	Mint Mark	M	C
761	7	B	MARS VICTOR. Mars adv. r., with spear and trophy.	1	I	322
762	2	HH	MARTI CONSERVATORI. Mars standing r., holding spear and leaning on shield.	3	II	N
763	5	B	As preceding.	3	II	338
764	11	C	,,	3	II	341
765	9	B	MARTI CONSERVATORI. Mars facing, head l., otherwise as preceding.	9	IV	352
766	7	B	MARTI PACIF. Mars adv. l., with olive-branch, spear and shield.	1	I	356
767	11	B	MARTI PATRI PROPVG. Mars adv. r., with spear and shield.	1	I	363

No.	Obv. Legend	Obv. Type	Reverse	Mint Mark	M	C
768	12	B	As preceding.	1	I	364
769	—	—	P M TR P COS II P P. Female figure seated l., on double cornucopiae, holding sceptre.	3 or 4	II	397
770	11	B	PRINCIPI IVVENTVTIS. Emperor l., holding two standards.	1	I	444
771	4	HH	As preceding.	4	II	N
772	5	B	,,	4	II	449
773	5	HH	,,	4	II	N
774	2	B	PRINCIPI IVVENTVTIS. Emperor l., with globe and spear.	4	II	427
775	2	HH	As preceding.	4	II	428 & 433
776	5	B	,,	4	II	429
777	5	BB	,,	4	II	N
778	4	B	,,	4	II	431
779	5	HH	,,	4	II	436
780	5	B	PRINCIPI IVVENTVTIS. Emperor r., with spear and globe.	3	II	418
781	11	B	As preceding.	3	II	N

No.	Obv. Legend	Obv. Type	Reverse	Mint Mark	M	C
782	9	B	As preceding.	9	IV	N

No.	Obv. Legend	Obv. Type	Reverse	Mint Mark	M	C
783	1 or 2	A	PROVIDENTIAE AVGG. Gateway, as illustration.	14	VII	454

No.	Obv. Legend	Obv. Type	Reverse	Mint Mark	M	C
783a	7	B	ROMAE AETER. Roma seated l. in hexastyle temple, with sceptre and globe.	1	I	N
784	5	B	ROMAE AETER AVGG. Roma seated l., holding branch and globe.	3	II	468
785	4	HH	ROMAE RESTITVTAE. Type as preceding	3	II	474
786	4	B	As preceding.	3	II	N
787	5	B	,,	3	II	475
788	1 or 2	A	SARMATIA DEVICTA. Victory r., holding trophy and palm, foot on captive.	15	VI	487
789	5	B	SECVRITAS AVGG. Securitas standing l., r. hand to head, leaning on pillar.	3	II	491
790	4	HH	As preceding.	3	II	492
791	9	B	SOLI INVICTO COMITI. Sol standing l., raising r. hand and holding globe.	9	IV	530
792	4	B	As preceding.	10	IV	524
793	9	B	,,	10	IV	530
794	4	B	,,	11	IV	524
795	9	B	,,	11	IV	530
796	2	C	,,	12	IV	521
797	9	B	,,	12	IV	530
798	8	B	,,	12	IV	N
799	4	B	,,	13	IV	524
800	4	BB	,,	13	IV	N
801	9	OO	,,	13	IV	533
802	5	B	,,	2	V	525
803	4	B	,,	5	V	524

No.	Obv. Legend	Obv. Type	Reverse	Mint Mark	M	C
804	5	B	As preceding.	4	II	525
805	5	B	,,	3	II	525
806	12	B	,,	3	II	536
807	11	B	,,	3	II	534
808	2	C	,,	6	IV	521
809	2	HH	,,	6	IV	523
810	5	B	,,	6	IV	525
811	9	B	,,	6	IV	530
812	11	C	,,	6	IV	534
813	12	B	,,	6	IV	536
814	4	B	,,	7	V	524
815	11	B	,,	8	III	534
816	12	B	,,	8	III	536
817	12	C	,,	8	III	536
818	2	C	,,	8	IV	521
819	4	C	,,	8	IV	524
820	5	B	,,	8	IV	525
821	11	B	,,	8	IV	534
822	12	B	,,	8	IV	536
823	4	B	SOLI INVICTO COMITI. Sol. in quadriga l., with globe and whip.	13	IV	547
824	5	B	SPES REIPVBL. Emperor on horseback l., with spear ; to l., captive.	4	II	553
825	2	HH	SPES REPVBLICAE. Same type, without captive.	4	II	555

No.	OBV. LEGEND	OBV. TYPE	REVERSE	MINT MARK	M	C
826	2	D	VICTORIAE LAETAE PRINC PERP. Two Victories placing shield inscr. VOT P R on altar.	17or18	VI	631
827	2	D	As preceding.	18	VI	631

828	2	E	As preceding.	1	VI	633
829	6 or 6A	E	,,	1	VI	635
830	9	HH, no shield	,,	1	VI	638
831	8	,,	,,	1	VI	638 v.
832	10 or 10A	E	,,	1	VI	640
833	1 or 2	D	VIRTVS EXERCIT. Standard inscr. VOT XX between two seated captives.	1 or 14	VI	695

Helena

First wife of Constantius Chlorus and mother of Constantine the Great.

834 FL HELENA AVGVSTA. Bust of Helena r.

℞. SECVRITAS REIPVBLICE. Securitas veiled, standing l., holding branch: in ex., PLON. *C.* 12. *M.* vi.

Fausta

Daughter of Maximianus Herculeus and wife of Constantine the Great.

835 FLAV MAX FAVSTA AG or AVG. Bust of Fausta r.

℞. SALVS REIPVBLICAE. Fausta, veiled, standing l., holding two children: in ex., PLON. *C.* 7. *M.* vii.

Crispus.

Eldest son of Constantine the Great: created Caesar in 317, and put to death by his father's orders in 326 A.D.

Obverse Legends:—

    1 CRISPVS NOB CAES

    2 CRISPVS NOBIL C

    3 D N CRISPO NOB CAES

    4 FL IVL CRISPVS NOB CAES

    5 IVL CRISPVS NOB C

836	2	D	BEATA TRANQVILLITAS. Altar inscr. VOTIS XX, surmounted by globe and three stars.	14 or 19	VI	12
837	2	DD	As preceding.	14	VI	13
837a	2	GG	,,	14	VI	11
838	2	DD	,,	16	VI	13
838a	2	DD	,,	20	VI	13
839	2	HH	BEAT TRANQLITAS. Type as preceding.	14	VI	28

No.	Obv. Legend	Obv. Type	Reverse	Mint Mark	M	C
840	2	GG	As preceding.	14	VI	27
840a	2	GG	,,	16or20	VI	27
841	2	DD	,,	14	VI	29
842	2	D or G	,,	14	VI	N
843	2	HH	,,	16	VI	28
844	2	DD	,,	16	VI	29

No.	Obv. Legend	Obv. Type	Reverse	Mint Mark	M	C
845	5	A	CAESARVM NOSTRORVM. Wreath enclosing VOT X.	15	VI	44
846	1	B	CLARITAS REIPVBLICAE. Sol standing l., raising r. hand and holding globe.	7	V	51
847	1	B	PRINCIPIA IVVENTVTIS. Crispus standing r., leaning on shield and holding spear.	2	V	105
848	4	B	PROVIDENTIAE CAESS. Gateway, as on no. 783.	14	VII	124
849	1	B	SOLI INVICTO COMITI. Type as no. 846	7	V	136
850	4	B	As preceding.	7	V	137
851	1	B	,,	2	V	136
852	4	B	,,	2	V	137
853	1	B	VICTORIAE LAETAE PRINC PERP. Two Victories placing shield inscr. VOT P R on altar.	1	VI	148
854	4	E	As preceding.	1	VI	151
855	3	B	,,	17	VI	155
856	1	B	,,	18	VI	156
857	3	B	,,	18	VI	155

No.	Obv. Legend	Obv. Type	Reverse	Mint Mark	M	C
858	1	D	VIRTVS EXERCIT. Standard inscr. VOT X X between two seated captives.	1	VI	179
859	2	D	As preceding.	1	VI	173

Constantine II.

Second son of Constantine the Great and Fausta. Caesar 317-337. Augustus 337-340 A.D.

Obverse legends :—

1 CONSTANTINVS IVN N C
2 CONSTANTINVS IVN NOB C
3 D N CONSTANTINO IVN NOB C
4 FL CL CONSTANTINVS IVN N C
5 CONSTANTINVS IVN NOBIL C

No.	Obv. Legend	Obv. Type	Reverse	Mint Mark	M	C
860	1	PP or RR	BEATA TRANQVILLITAS. Type as no. 836.	14	VI	16
861	1	PP	As preceding.	16	VI	16
861a	1	PP	,,	20	VI	16
862	1	D	BEAT TRANQLITAS. Type as preceding.	14	VI	9
863	1	DD	,,	14or16	VI	10
863a	1	P	,,	16	VI	N
863b	1	JJ, but no helmet	,,	14	VI	N
864	1	RR	,,	16or20	VI	8
864b	1	S	,,	16	VI	N
865	2	A	CAESARVM NOSTRORVM. As no. 845	15	VI	38
866	5	A	As preceding.	15	VI	N
867	2	B	PROVIDENTIAE CAESS. Type as no. 783	14	VII	164
868	1	B	SOLI INVICTA COMITI. Sol standing l., raising r. hand and holding globe.	7	V	183
869	4	C	As preceding.	7	V	186
870	4	C	,,	2	V	186

871	4	C	As preceding.	5	V	186
872	1	SS	VICTORIAE LAETAE PRINC PERP. Two Victories placing shield inscr. VOT P R on altar.	1	VI	219
873	4	SS	As preceding.	1	VI	224
874	3	C	,,	17	VI	227
875	1	SS	,,	18	VI	219
876	4	SS	,,	18	VI	225
877	3	P	,,	18	VI	N
878	1	RR	VIRTVS EXERCIT. Standard inscr. VOT X X between two seated captives.	1	VI	252
879	1	RR	As preceding.	14	VI	252

880	1	SS	VIRTVS EXERCIT. Trophy between two seated captives.	14	VI	262

Constantius II

Third son of Constantine the Great and Fausta. Caesar 323-337; Augustus 337-361.

881 FL IVL CONSTANTIVS NOB C. Laur., dr. and cuir. bust of Constantius r.
℞. PROVIDENTIAE CAESS. Gateway as on no. 783 : in ex., PLON. C. 168.
M. vii.

882 As preceding, but bust l. C. 169. M. vii.

883 FLA CONSTANTIVS NOB C. Laur., dr. and cuir. bust r.
℞. as preceding. C. 171 *var.* M. vii.

73

Chapter X. The Last Coins of Roman Britain.

On the death of Constantine the Great in 337 A.D., the empire was divided between his sons. Constantine II received Gaul, Britain and Spain, and Constans Italy, the Danubian provinces and Africa. Thrace, Macedonia, Greece and the East were allotted to Constantius II. In 340 war broke out between Constantine II and Constans which ended in the defeat of the former and his death at Aquileia. Thus all the Western portion of the empire fell to Constans. About this time the Picts and Scots began once more to make raids on the northern part of Roman Britain, and Constans found it necessary to visit the island in the winter of 342-3. To induce the invaders to keep the peace he made some kind of a treaty with them, probably allowing some of them to settle in Roman territory.

In 350 a revolt in Gaul caused the murder of Constans, and a soldier named Flavius Magnus Magnentius was raised to the purple. He was of Gaulish or British descent, and had been brought up in the household of Constans. The civil commotion in Gaul consequent upon Magnentius' elevation seems to have had an effect upon the coinage used in Britain, remembering that there was now no official British mint in operation and that all supplies of coin had to be brought to the island from Gaul. About this time, therefore, the first of the " barbarous 4th century " coins may have been struck. These are usually copies of the well-known FEL TEMP REPARATIO coins which were first issued about 348 A.D., the commonest reverse type of the series being a soldier advancing l., striking downwards with his spear at a fallen barbarian horseman. The workmanship of the barbarous copies varies from good to grotesque, probably according to the skill of the die-cutter, or the lack of it, and most of the pieces are overstruck on earlier coins of the Constantinian period. Some, indeed, are struck over official coins of FEL TEMP REPARATIO types. These " barbarous 4th century " coins apparently continued to be issued until the beginning of the 5th century or even later, the style and fabric becoming more and more degraded.

Further evidence of the decline of official authority in Britain is provided by the coins of Carausius II, the first-known of which was the subject of a paper by Sir Arthur Evans in 1887 (*Num. Chron.*, 3rd Series, Vol. VII, pp. 191 ff.). The piece is illustrated here, and in the description the various ligatured and reversed letters of the legends have been resolved into normal form.

884 DOMINO CARAVSIO CES. Diademed bust of Carausius r.
R. DOMIN CONTA. Emperor standing l. in galley, holding phoenix and standard : Victory seated l. at the helm. Æ size as illustration.
Found at Richborough, and formerly in the Evans collection : now in the Ashmolean Museum.

Dr. C. H. V. Sutherland, in *Num. Chron.*, 6th Series, Vol. V, 1945, has given a study of this and four other coins on the similar legends and also of the following piece :—

884a DOMINO CA — — CENSERIS. Diademed bust r.
R. Soldier adv. l., spearing fallen horseman.
Æ, 18 mm. diameter. *Found at Richborough and now in the British Museum.*

In addition to the six coins dealt with by Dr. Sutherland, Mr. Philip V. Hill, in *Num. Chron.*, 6th Series, Vol. VIII, 1948, gives details of three more " Carausius II " coins in the collection of Mr. Fred Baldwin. It is possible that other pieces of this class may come to light from time to time, and it might be well for collectors carefully to scrutinise their barbarous and overstruck coins of this period with a view to locating additional specimens.

Dr. Sutherland suggests, in the paper cited above, that these coins were issued by petty chieftains at the time of Magnentius' usurpation, or soon after, when official rule in Britain might have been temporarily weakened, and that the reverse legends may be a prudent admission of the supreme authority of Constantius II who in 353 put an end to Magnentius' brief tenure of the western empire. There seems little doubt that at this period there were opportunities for partial autonomy, and if the Carausius II of these coins was a grandson of the admiral-emperor—which is not impossible—he may have inherited some of his grandfather's energy and initiative. Any chieftain who thus set himself up as a junior colleague of the legitimate ruler might be expected to advertise his newly-won semi-independence by an issue of coins, and no doubt the quickest way to produce such a coinage was by overstriking pieces already in circulation. Two of the coins dealt with by Dr. Sutherland, and one of those cited by Mr. Hill, are certainly overstruck on earlier coins.

About two years after the suppression of Magnentius, Constantius II, now master of the whole empire, appointed his cousin Julian to be Caesar for the Gallic provinces. Early in 360 Julian received news that the Picts and Scots had broken the agreement they had made with Constans and were attacking the frontier districts, and he therefore despatched an army under Lupicinus to drive them out. The attempt was only partially successful, and Lupicinus' campaign in Britain was cut short by the troubles arising from Julian being proclaimed Augustus in 360 by his troops, who had revolted against Constantius. In 364 Britain was being attacked by Picts, Scots, Saxons and other raiders, and in 368 the treachery of the local levies who garrisoned the Wall destroyed any effectiveness that the system of fortifications might have retained. Picts from the north, Scots from the west, and Franks and Saxons landing in the south-east, entirely over-ran the province, and such forces as the government could put in the field were completely routed, Nectaridus, count of the Saxon shore, and Fullofaudes, duke of Britain, being killed.

Valentinian I (364-375), who at that time was emperor of the west, was unable to come himself to Britain to deal with the invaders, but instead sent Count Theodosius, a skilled and experienced general, with a large army, to restore the situation. Landing at Richborough, Theodosius advanced on London, finding the country terrorised by bands of plunderers. He made London his headquarters for the winter, reorganized the government, and in the spring began to take order with the invading marauders. In due course he reached the Wall and restored it and its forts, and also ordered the construction of signal stations on the Yorkshire coast. The stations were designed to prolong northward the chain of Saxon shore forts, and it is probable that they could quickly transmit to York, by some system of signals, news of any attempted raid from the sea.

We may assume that in this troubled period the production of both " barbarous radiates " and " barbarous fourth-century " coins was continued here and there. Even in hazardous and uncertain times small change is necessary, and there would be little infiltration of official issues from the continent.

Theodosius' services to the empire were requited in a way typical of the times : he was murdered by order of Valens (364-375), the colleague of Valentinian I. In the British campaign had also served Theodosius the Younger (son of the murdered general, and later Theodosius I) and Magnus Clemens Maximus, and it is to the career of the latter we must now turn.

Maximus, who was of Spanish descent, remained in Britain after its pacification, and attained high rank. He campaigned successfully against the Picts and Scots, who, despite their defeat by Theodosius, continued to be troublesome. In 383 he rebelled against Gratian (367-383) and made himself emperor of Britain and later, after defeating Gratian near Paris, of Gaul and Spain. But to gain these victories he had to withdraw so many fighting men from Britain that the province once more became the prey of invaders, and the northern barbarians overwhelmed the Wall defences for the last time. They were never rebuilt ; and although a coin of Valentinian II (383-392) found in the fort of Chesterholm-Vindolanda* may indicate some kind of temporary occupation after 383, its evidence is not conclusive.

Magnus Maximus has been credited with the re-opening of the London mint, and indeed it is logical to suppose that a mint would be amongst his earliest requirements. Unfortunately the coins now to be described do not bear the mint-mark LON in any form, but have AVG instead. London had certainly been given the title AVGVSTA about this time, perhaps in celebration of Theodosius' victories, but the experts have not yet agreed that the mint-mark AVG must refer to London.

885   D N MAG MA XIMVS P F AVG.   Diademed bust of Maximus r.

    R.   RESTITVTOR REIPVBLICAE.   Emperor standing holding labarum and Victory on globe : in ex., AVG.

    N solidus. Cf. C. 4. In the Copenhagen collection.

886   *Obv.* as preceding.

    R.   VOT V MVLT X in wreath : below, AVG.

    AR siliqua. From the North Mendip hoard (Num. Chron., 4th Series, Vol. XV, 1915).

887   D N MAG MA XIMVS P F AVG.   Diademed bust r.

    R.   VICTORIA AVGG.   Two emperors seated facing, holding globe : behind, half-length figure of Victory facing : in ex., AVGOB.

    N solidus. C.g. British Museum.

888   *Obv.* as preceding.

    R.   VICTORIA AVGG.   Victory adv. l., with wreath and palm : in ex., AVGPS.

    AR siliqua. From the North Mendip hoard.

---

* See Archaeologia Aeliana, 4th Series, Vol. XIII, 1936, p. 228.

The use of AVGG in the reverse legends of Nos. 887 and 888 would indicate that Maximus was claiming to be the legal colleague of Theodosius I, emperor in the east, and the following coin may have been struck by Maximus for similar propaganda reasons :—

889 D N THEODO SIVS P F AVG.   Diademed and dr. bust of Theodosius r.

R̟. as No. 887.

N̟ solidus (actually silver gilt). *British Museum.*

As has been said above, the attribution of these five coins to the mint of London has not found general acceptance, and in 1947 the case for the opposition was well stated by Dr. Friedrich Mayreder. In his paper " Londinium or Augustodunum " (*Num. Chron.*, 6th Series, Vol. VII, p. 122-125) the evidence was re-examined, and the conclusion reached that Augustodunum was the actual mint-place of the coins under review. With this conclusion the present writer finds it difficult to disagree, as he has never been satisfied with the attribution to London. Besides, if Maximus had re-opened the London mint, might we not expect to find some bronze pieces issued at the same time ? Yet none has been recorded, and it seems unlikely that Maximus would have lost the propaganda value of a bronze issue if he had had so convenient a mint for its production. This is not, of course, conclusive, as every collector knows how much easier it is to acquire a *siliqua* of Maximus than one of his bronze coins ; but it is a point that should be borne in mind.

In 388 Maximus, driven either by ambition or the force of circumstances, invaded Italy, the young Valentinian II (383-392) fleeing at his approach and appealing for aid to Theodosius. The latter took up his cause and marched against Maximus, whom he defeated and afterwards executed. After his fall, Britain must have remained the prey of the barbarians for some years, until Stilicho was able, about 395, to reorganise the defences. Stilicho, the great vandal general, had been appointed by Theodosius to be regent for the young Honorius, his son, now emperor of the west, and his defeats of the Picts and Saxons were celebrated in a poem by Claudian which was written in 399, and in another datable to 400. But the respite was of short duration, as in 401 or 402 Stilicho had to withdraw troops from Britain for use against the Goths. In 406 the remaining forces in Britain, in an attempt to safeguard the country, elected one Marcus as emperor. The latter was soon murdered, and was followed by another usurper named Gratian, the reign of the latter only lasting four months. Next the army raised a soldier called Constantine to the purple, chiefly because of his name, and this ruler, whom we know as Constantine III, was acknowledged by Honorius as his colleague. Constantine made such arrangements as he could for the defence of the island, and crossed over to Gaul to secure the threatened Rhine frontier, but he must have actually weakened the British garrison by taking troops with him.

In 410 the Romano-Britons, feeling that the emperor they had created was neglecting them, revolted against Constantine, expelled his governors, and appealed to Honorius for aid whilst asserting their loyalty to him. Honorius, however, had already too much trouble nearer home, and all he did was to send instructions to the islanders to arrange for their own defence as best they might. After this we can be certain of little. It is recorded that when St. Germanus visited Britain in 429 he led some local militia against a body of barbarian invaders and defeated them ; and in 446 the Romano-Britains appealed to Aetius, then consul at Rome for the third time, for help, but in vain. The link between Britain and Rome is thus shown to be gradually becoming more tenuous after 410, and when the actual break took place is a matter that has not yet been agreed on.

The coinage of this last phase of Roman Britain consists entirely of small barbarous copper coins. Such official coins as are found on sites of the period are from
continental mints. Many of the larger coins show evidences of clipping, as indeed
do many *siliquae* found in late hoards in Britain. No doubt scarcity of silver and
copper accounts for this clipping, as the copper would be wanted to produce further
coins, and the silver, though not needed for coinage, would have a bullion value.
Apparently the limit of degradation of the coinage was reached by the makers of
the tiny pieces found at Lydney Park, Glos. Excavations made in 1928-29 and
reported in the Society of Antiquaries Research Committee's Report, No. IX, 1932,
produced two hoards of coins. One of these consisted chiefly of pieces from Constantine I to Magnentius, including many barbarous and overstruck coins, and
may have been deposited *c.* 365-370. The other was made up of 1,646 coins,
fragments of coins, and pieces of corroded bronze. There was not a single complete
specimen of a regular copper coin or of an equivalent barbarous copy, but many
clippings or fragments of such coins. The hoard, however, consisted mostly of
minimi of, apparently four denominations. The largest averaged 7½ *mm.* in diameter, the smallest ranged between 2.5 and 3 *mm.* and fifty-one of these could be
spread without difficulty on an ordinary halfpenny. Such obverse types as are
recognisable throughout the four classes appear to be diademed heads, and the
reverses of all are copies of the FEL TEMP REPARATIO, " soldier spearing fallen horseman," type. The style, if one may use the word, of all the coins is bad, but of the
smallest almost unbelievably so. The date of the hoard, as suggested by the
Report, must be in the fifth century ; and it is safe to assume that the deposition
must have taken place at almost the same time as the last vestiges of Roman rule
in Britain were dying out.

With these tiny coins of Lydney it is proposed to close this brief survey of the
coinage of Roman Britain. The question of the issue of any coinage in the " Dark
Ages " of Britain, *c.* 450-600 A.D., is still in dispute, but it would be inaccurate to
apply to such coinage the name " Romano-British." Whatever the status of Britain
at this time, few vestiges, if any, of Roman authority can have remained, and we
may visualise the former prosperous province as a " debateable land " where the
Britons fought with less and less success against the rising tide of invasion. The
character of the invasion, too, was changing, and instead of raids by plunderers
the inhabitants had to struggle against increasing numbers of incomers whose
intention was to settle on the lands they over-ran ; and thus began the England of
the Anglo-Saxons.

Chapter XI: Bibliography.

The bibliography of Roman Britain and of Roman coinage is enormous. Both are fields where new books and articles are continually appearing, and also where many of the older published works still have a value, use and interest in modern studies. A bibliography in a book such as this cannot in any way be fully comprehensive of all the publications in the field, available space alone is against it. Here an endeavour is made to be sufficiently indicative, with the added annotations in places, to give the reader enough guidance to further their studies on the broader front as well as, at times, in greater detail. The latest information is always to be found in the periodical literature, often appearing even several years before its publication in a book, and for anyone anxious to keep abreast of developments in thought and new finds regular reading of the periodicals in the subject field is a necessity.

Numismatics

AKERMAN, J. Y. *Coins of the Romans relating to Britain.* London, 1836; 3rd ed. 1844 (of antiquarian interest as an early attempt at an evaluation of the series).

BASTIEN, P. and METZGER, C. *Le trésor de Beaurains (dit d'Arras).* Wetteren, Belgium, 1976 (meticulous publication of the major hoard that contained the Arras medallion).

BURNETT, A. *The Coins of Roman Britain.* British Museum Keys to the Past. London, 1977 (a useful short guide).

CARSON, R. A. G. 'Bronze medallions of Carausius', *British Museum Quarterly* 37, pts. 1–2 (1973), pp. 1–4.

———— 'Mints and Coinage of Carausius and Allectus', *Journal of the British Archaeological Association* XXII, pp. 36ff.

———— *Principal Coins of the Romans. Vol. 2: The Principate, 31 BC–AD 296.* London, 1980 (includes many pieces relating to Britain, and the Carausius and Allectus issues).

CARSON, R. A. G., HILL, P. V., and KENT, J. P. C. *Late Roman Bronze Coinage, AD 324–498.* London, 1960, new impression 1978 (detailed investigation and chronological ordering of issues under individual mints).

CASEY, P. J. (ed.). *The End of Roman Britain.* Oxford, 1979 (symposium papers; note especially Casey's paper on 'Magnus Maximus in Britain', pp. 66–79).

CASEY, P. J. and REECE, R. (eds.). *Coins and the Archaeologist.* Oxford, 1974 (symposium papers, including six on coinage and Roman Britain).

C = COHEN, H. *Description Historique des Monnaies frappées sous l'Empire Romain.* 8 vols. 2nd ed. Paris, 1880–92; reprinted London, 1955.

GENEBRIER, D. M. *Histoire de Carausius, empereur de la Grande-Bretagne, etc.* Paris, 1840.

GNECCHI, F. *I medaglioni romani.* 3 vols. Milan, 1912.

GRANT, M. *Roman History from Coins.* Cambridge, 1958.

HILL, P. V. *"Barbarous Radiates": Imitations of Third Century Roman Coins.* American Numismatic Society Notes & Monographs No. 112. New York, 1949.

———— *The Coinage of Septimius Severus and his Family of the Mint of Rome, AD 193–217.* London, 1964.

———— *The Undated Coins of Rome, AD 98–148.* London, 1970 (both books, in postulating a precise chronology for the periods concerned, establish the dates of many of the coins that refer to Britain).

KENT, J. P. C. and HIRMER, M. *Roman Coins.* London, 1978 (magnificently illustrated survey, including many coins relating to Roman Britain, with invaluable commentary in text).

KENT, J. P. C. and PAINTER, K. S. *Wealth of the Roman World.* London, 1977 (British Museum special exhibition that included several treasures from Roman Britain and exhibited 531 coins of the Roman and associated worlds).

M & S see ROMAN IMPERIAL COINAGE.

MATTINGLY, H. *Coins of the Roman Empire in the British Museum:* Vol. V. *Pertinax to Elagabalus.* 2nd ed. London, 1976 (incorporates much new work on the Severan issues by Dr P. V. Hill).

MATTINGLY, H. and STEBBING, W. P. B. *The Richborough Hoard of Radiates.* American Numismatic Society Notes & Monographs No. 80. New York, 1938.

PAINTER, K. S. *The Water Newton Early Christian Silver.* London, 1977 (Appendix B on the Water Newton 1974 hoard of gold solidi).

ROMAN IMPERIAL COINAGE, edited by H. Mattingly, E. A. Sydenham, C. H. V. Sutherland, and R. A. G. Carson. London.
 I. *Augustus to Vitellius.* 1923.
 II. *Vespasian to Hadrian.* 1926.
 III. *Antoninus Pius to Commodus.* 1930.
 IV. 1. *Pertinax to Geta.* 1936.
   2. *Macrinus to Pupienus.* 1938.
   3. *Gordian III to Uranius Antoninus.* 1949.
 V. 1. *Valerian to Florian.* 1927.
   2. *Probus to Amandus.* 1933.
 IV. *Diocletian's Reform to Death of Maximinus.* 1967.
 VII. *Constantine and Licinius.* 1966.
 VIII. *Sons of Constantine to Death of Jovian* (in the press).
 IX. *Valentinian I to Theodosius I.* 1951.
 X. *Death of Theodosius I to Reform of Anastasius* (forthcoming).
SHIEL. N. *The Episode of Carausius and Allectus: the Literary and Numismatic Evidence.* Oxford, 1977 (a most detailed account of the many problems and questions relating to the period).
STUKELEY, W. *Medallic History of Marcus Aurelius Valerius Carausius, Emperor in Britain.* London, 1747 (although highly unreliable it is of interest as an indication of the contemporary approach to numismatics from the pen of the clergyman who peopled Stonehenge with Druids).
SUTHERLAND, C. H. V. *Coinage in Roman Imperial Policy, 31 BC–AD 68.* London, 1951.
―――― *Coinage and Currency in Roman Britain.* Oxford, 1937 (seminal standard work on the subject).
―――― *Romano-British Imitations of Bronze Coins of Claudius I.* American Numismatic Society Notes & Monographs No. 65. New York, 1935.
TOYNBEE. J. M. C. *Roman Medallions.* New York, 1944.
WEBB, P. H. *Reign and Coinage of Carausius.* London, 1908 (ex. *Numismatic Chronicle* 4th ser. vol. VII, 1907).

Roman Britain

BIRLEY, A. R. *Life in Roman Britain.* London, 1976 (a good introductory account).
―――― *Septimius Severus: the African Emperor.* London, 1971.
BIRLEY, E. *Roman Britain and the Roman Army.* Kendal, 1961 (collection of essays on various aspects).
BOON. G. C. *Silchester: The Roman Town of Calleva.* 2nd ed. Newton Abbot, 1974 (detailed evaluation of the most thoroughly excavated Roman town in Britain).
BRITISH MUSEUM. *Guide to the Antiquities of Roman Britain.* 2nd ed. London, 1958.
BURKE, J. *Life in the Villa in Roman Britain.* London, 1978.
BURN. A. R. *Agricola and Roman Britain.* London, 1953 (still a useful concise guide).
―――― *The Romans in Britain: an anthology of inscriptions.* Oxford, 1932.
BUSHE-FOX, J. P. *Excavations at Richborough.* Society of Antiquaries Research Reports, nos. 6, 7, 10, 16, 23. London. Vol. 1, 1926; Vol. 2, 1928; Vol. 3, 1932; Vol. 4, 1949; Vol. 5, edited by B. W. Cunliffe, 1968.
CLAYTON, P. A. *Archaeological Sites of Britain.* London, 1976 (includes prehistoric as well as Roman sites, and illustrates several coins).
―――― (ed.). *A Companion to Roman Britain.* Oxford, 1980 (includes among the basic aspects of Roman Britain section on the economy and coinage, and a detailed gazetteer of sites).
COLLINGWOOD, R. G. and MYRES, J. N. L. *Roman Britain and the English Settlements.* 2nd ed. Oxford, repr. 1956.
COLLINGWOOD, R. G. and RICHMOND, I. A. *The Archaeology of Roman Britain.* Rev. ed. London, 1969.
COLLINGWOOD, R. G. and WRIGHT, R. P. *The Roman Inscriptions of Britain: 1. Inscriptions on Stone.* Oxford, 1965 (essential source book that supercedes *Corpus Inscriptionum Latinorum (CIL)* Vol. VII; heavily illustrated with detailed discussion of inscriptions, provenances, etc.).
CRAWFORD, O. G. S. *Topography of Roman Scotland North of the Antonine Wall.* Cambridge, 1949.
CUNLIFFE. B. W. *Excavations at Portchester Castle, Vol. 1: Roman.* Society of Antiquaries Research Reports no. 32. London, 1975.
―――― *Fishbourne: A Roman Palace and its Garden.* London, 1971 (excavation of what was probably the palace of Cogidumnus, the client king of Rome, near Chichester).
―――― *Roman Bath.* Society of Antiquaries Research Reports no. 24. London, 1969.
DUDLEY, D. R. and WEBSTER, G. *The Roman Conquest of Britain AD 43–57.* London, 1965.
FRERE. S. S. *Britannia: A History of Roman Britain.* 3rd ed. London, 1978.
―――― *Verulamium Excavations, Vol. 1.* Society of Antiquaries Research Reports no. 28. London, 1972.
HORSLEY. Revd J. *Britannia Romana.* London, 1732 ('If a student of Roman Britain chooses to ignore Horsley, he will do so at his peril' – Sir George Macdonald).
HULL. M. R. *Roman Colchester.* Society of Antiquaries Research Reports no. 20. London, 1958.
JOHNSON. S. *The Roman Forts of the Saxon Shore.* London, 1976.

JOHNSTONE, D. E. (ed.). *The Saxon Shore*. London, 1977 (symposium papers on all aspects of this late Roman coastal fortification).

LIVERSIDGE, J. *Britain in the Roman Empire*. London, 1973 (detailed account of most aspects of life in Roman Britain).

LONDON MUSEUM. *London in Roman Times*. London Museum catalogue no. 3. London, 1946.

MERRIFIELD, R. *The Roman City of London*. London, 1965 (in depth survey with gazetteer of finds).

MOORE, R. W. *The Romans in Britain: a selection of Latin texts*. London, 1938 (useful guide to original sources from Latin authors in the original, and excerpts from Greek authors in translation).

NASH-WILLIAMS, V. E. *The Roman Frontier in Wales*. Rev. ed. by M. G. Jarrett. Cardiff, 1969.

ORDNANCE SURVEY. *Map of Roman Britain*. New ed. Chessington, 1979.

PEROWNE, S. *Hadrian*. London, 1960 (excellent biography of the emperor closely concerned with Britain).

RICHMOND, I. A. *Roman Britain*. Pelican History of Britain, vol. 1. 2nd ed. Harmondsworth, 1963.

────── (ed.). *Roman and Native in North Britain*. Edinburgh, 1958.

RIVET, A. L. F. *Town and Country in Roman Britain*. London, 1964.

────── (ed.). *The Roman Villa in Britain*. London, 1969.

ROYAL COMMISSION ON HISTORICAL MONUMENTS. *Eburacum: Roman York*. London, 1962 (Vol. 1 of the inventory of the historical monuments of York).

────── *Roman London*. London, 1928 (Vol. III of the inventory of the historical monuments of London).

SCULLARD, H. H. *Roman Britain: Outpost of Empire*. London, 1979.

TACITUS. *Agricola and the Germania*. trans. by H. Mattingly. Harmondsworth, 1948 (basic classical account by the father-in-law of the Governor of Britain).

WACHER, J. *Roman Britain*. London, 1978.

────── *The Towns of Roman Britain*. London, 1978 (an invaluable detailed survey).

WEBSTER, G. *Boudica: The British Revolt against Rome, AD 60*. London, 1978.

────── *The Roman Imperial Army*. 2nd ed. London, 1979.

WHEELER, R. E. M. and WHEELER, T. V. *Excavations at Lydney Park, Gloucestershire*. Society of Antiquaries Research Report no. 9. London, 1932 (site of the famous Lydney hoard find of tiny late Roman coins).

────── *Excavations at Verulamium*. Society of Antiquaries Research Report no. 11. London, 1936.

WILSON, R. J. A. *A Guide to the Roman Remains in Britain*. London, 1975.

Hadrian's Wall

BIRLEY, E. *Research on Hadrian's Wall*. Kendal, 1961 (examines many aspects of problems on the Wall, its anatomy, the forts, etc., their past interpretations and present state of research, with detailed references).

BREEZE, D. J. and DOBSON, B. *Hadrian's Wall*. Rev. ed. Harmondsworth, 1978 (most recent and useful assessment of the various aspects of the Wall and its garrisons).

BRUCE, J. COLLINGWOOD. *Handbook to the Roman Wall*. 13th ed., edited and enlarged by Charles Daniels. Newcastle upon Tyne, 1978 (the 'bible' of all guides, whose first edition appeared in 1863).

DIVINE, D. *The North-West Frontier of Rome: A Military Study of Hadrian's Wall*. London, 1969.

JONES, G. D. B. *Hadrian's Wall from the Air*. Warminster, 1976 (available with a set of 16 35mm colour slides).

ORDNANCE SURVEY. Large scale maps of *Hadrian's Wall*. Chessington, 1964; and *The Antonine Wall*. Chessington, 1969.

Periodicals: Archaeologia Aeliana (Society of Antiquaries of Newcastle upon Tyne), and *Transactions of the Cumberland and Westmorland Antiquarian and Archaeological Society*.

Periodicals

The premier annual numismatic publications are the *Numismatic Chronicle* of the Royal Numismatic Society, and the *British Numismatic Journal* of the British Numismatic Society. Also of growing importance and use is *Coin Hoards* (1975–), published by the RNS. Amongst the monthly periodicals Seaby's *Coin & Medal Bulletin* and Spink's *Numismatic Circular* often publish articles or notes on new coin finds and/or new coin types for particular emperors. The annual archaeological periodicals that are important for Roman Britain are: *Britannia*; the *Antiquaries Journal* (Society of Antiquaries of London); the *Archaeological Journal* (Royal Archaeological Institute), and the *Journal of Roman Studies* (Society for the Promotion of Roman Studies).

P.A.C.

Appendix : The Governors of Roman Britain

Any list of the governors of Roman Britain owes much to the work of Professor Eric Birley (who compiled the list published in the original 1951 edition of this book). Since that date a more recent study has appeared by A. R. Birley, 'The Governors of Roman Britain', *Epigraphische Studien* 4 (1967), 163–202. I have compiled the following list from various sources and it is here reproduced from my book *A Companion to Roman Britain* (Oxford, 1980), by courtesy of Phaidon Press Ltd., Oxford.

GOVERNORS

43	Aulus Plautius
47	Publius Ostorius Scapula
51/2	Aulus Didius Gallus
57/8	Quintus Veranius
58/9	Caius Suetonius Paulinus
61	Publius Petronius Turpilianus
63	Marcus Trebellius Maximus
69	Marcus Vettius Bolanus
71	Quintus Petillius Cerialis
73/4	Sextus Iulius Frontinus
78	Cnaeus Iulius Agricola
96	Sallustius Lucullus
97/8	Publius Metilius Nepos
98	Titus Avidius Quietus
103	Lucius Neratius Marcellus
	Marcus Appius Bradua
	Quintus Pompeius Falco
122–124	Aulus Platorius Nepos
127–133	Sextus Iulius Severus
135	Publius Mummius Sisenna
139–142	Quintus Lollius Urbicus
146	Cnaeus Papirius Aelianus
158	Cnaeus Iulius Verus
161/2	Marcus Statius Priscus
163	Sextus Calpurnius Agricola
	Quintus Antistius Adventus
184	Ulpius Marcellus
185–190	Publius Helvius Pertinax
192–197	Decimus Clodius Septimius Albinus
	Decimus Clodius Septimius ALBINUS (195–197) (usurper emperor in Britain)
197	Virius Lupus
198	Marcus Antius Crescens
205	Caius Valerius Pudens
205–207	Lucius Alfenus Senecio
210	Aulus Triarius Rufinus
213	T. Caius Iulius Marcus
216	Marcus Antonius Gordianus

EMPERORS

Caius Octavius Thurinus = AUGUSTUS (27 BC–AD 14)
TIBERIUS Claudius Nero (14–37)
Caius Caesar = CALIGULA (37–41)
Tiberius CLAUDIUS Drusus (41–54)

NERO Claudius Caesar Drusus Germanicus (54–68)

Servius Sulpicius GALBA (68–15 Jan. 69)
Marcus Salvius OTHO (15 Jan.–17 April 69)
Aulus VITELLIUS (2 Jan. 69–21 Dec. 69)
Titus Flavius VESPASIANus (1 July 69–79)

TITUS Flavius Vespasianus (79–81)
Titus Flavius DOMITIANus (81–96)
Marcus Cocceius NERVA (96–98)

Marcus Ulpius TRAJANus (98–117)

Publius Aelius HADRIANus (117–138)

Titus Aurelius Fulvus Boionius Arrius ANTONINUS (PIUS) (138–161)

MARCUS Aelius AURELIUS Verus (161–180)
LUCIUS Aurelius VERUS (161–169)

Lucius Aelius Aurelius COMMODUS (177–192)

Publius Helvius PERTINAX (1 Jan.–28 March 193)
Marcus DIDIUS JULIANUS (28 March–1 June 193)
Caius PESCENNIUS NIGER (193–194)
Lucius SEPTIMIUS SEVERUS (193–211)

Marcus Aurelius Antoninus = CARACALLA (198–217)

Lucius (or Publius) Septimius GETA (209–212)

Marcus Opelius MACRINUS (217–218)
Marcus Aurelius Antoninus = ELAGABALUS (218–222)

219	Modius Iulius	
220	Tiberius Claudius Paulinus	
221/2	Marius Valerianus	Marcus Aurelius SEVERUS ALEXANDER (222–235)
223	T. Claudius Xenophon	
225	Maximus	
	Claudius Apellinus	
	Calvisius Rufus	
	Valerius Crescens	
	Fulvianus	
		Caius Iulius Verus MAXIMINUS (235–238)
237	Tuccianus	
		Marcus Antonius GORDIANus I and II (238)
		Decimus Caelius BALBINUS (238)
		Marcus Clodius PUPIENUS Maximus (238)
	Maecilius Fuscus	Marcus Antonius GORDIANus III (238–244)
	Egnatius Lucilianus	
242	Nonius Philippus	

Marcus Julius PHILIPpus I (244–249)
Marcus Julius PHILIPpus II (247–249)
Caius Messius Quintus TRAJANus DECIUS (249–251)
Caius Vibius TREBONIANUS GALLUS (251–253)
Caius Vibius Afinius Gallus Vendumnianus
VOLUSIANus (251–253)
Marcus Aemilius AEMILIANus (252–253)
Publius Licinius VALERIANus I (253–260)

THE GALLIC EMPIRE
Marcus Cassianus Latinius POSTUMUS (259–268)   Publius Licinius Egnatius GALLIENUS (253–268)
Ulpius Cornelius LAELIANUS (268)
Marcus Aurelius MARIUS (268)
Marcus Piavvonius VICTORINUS (268–270)   Marcus Aurelius CLAUDIUS II (268–270)
Caius Pius Esuvius TETRICUS I (270–273)   Lucius Domitius AURELIANus (270–275)
Caius Pius Esuvius TETRICUS II (270–273)

Marcus Claudius TACITUS (275–276)
Marcus Aurelius PROBUS (276–282)
Marcus Aurelius CARUS (282–283)
Marcus Aurelius NUMERIANus (283–284)
Marcus Aurelius CARINUS (283–285)
Caius Aurelius Valerius DIOCLETIANus (284–305)

THE BRITISH USURPER EMPERORS   Marcus Aurelius Valerius MAXIMIANUS (286–310)
Marcus Aurelius Mausaeus CARAUSIUS (287–293)
Caius ALLECTUS (293–296)

Flavius Valerius CONSTANTIUS I (305–306)
GALERIUS Valerius Maximianus (305–311)
Flavius Valerius SEVERUS II (306–307)
Galerius Valerius MAXIMINUS II (309–313)
Marcus Aurelius Valerius MAXENTIUS (306–312)
Valerius Licinianus LICINIUS I (308–324)
Flavius Valerius Constantinus = CONSTANTINE I,
the Great (307–337)
Flavius Claudius CONSTANTIN(E)us II (337–340)
Flavius Julius CONSTANS (337–350)
Flavius Julius CONSTANTIUS II (337–361)
(usurper emperor: Flavius Magnus MAGNENTIUS
(350–353)
Flavius Claudius JULIANus II (360–363)
Flavius JOVIANus (363–364)
Flavius VALENTINIANus I (364–373)
Flavius VALENS (364–378)
Flavius GRATIANus (367–383)
MAGNUS Clemens MAXIMUS (383–388)   Flavius VALENTINIANus II (373–392)
Flavius THEODOSIUS I (379–395)
FLAVIUS VICTOR (387–388; son of Magnus Maximus)
EUGENIUS (392–394)
CONSTANTINE III (407–411)   Flavius HONORIUS (393–423)
410   Britain officially notified to fend for itself

ROMAN WALLS

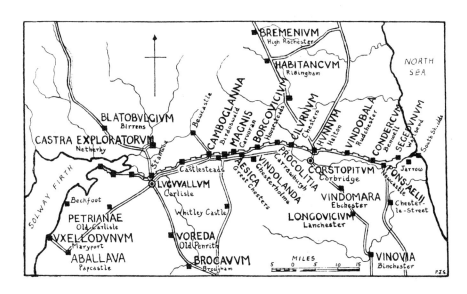

HADRIAN'S WALL

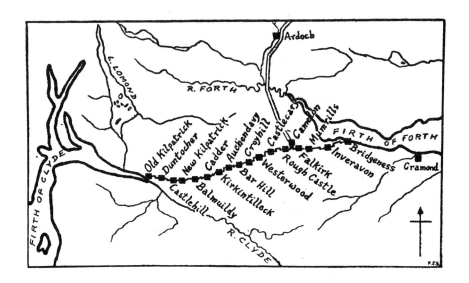

THE ANTONINE WALL

GENERAL INDEX

INDEX OF COIN TYPES

The figures given are the numbers of the coins in the catalogue and not the pages.